THE ECONOMICS OF TELEVISION

The Media, Culture and Society Series

Series editors: Richard Collins, James Curran, Nicholas Garnham, Paddy Scannell, Philip Schlesinger, Colin Sparks

The Economics of Television

The UK Case

Richard Collins
Nicholas Garnham
Gareth Locksley

SAGE Publications
London · Newbury Park · Beverly Hills · New Delhi

© Richard Collins, Nicholas Garnham and Gareth Locksley 1988
First published 1988

Published by Sage Publications Ltd
for *Media, Culture and Society*

SAGE Publications Ltd
28 Banner Street
London EC1Y 8QE

SAGE Publications Inc
2111 West Hillcrest Street
Newbury Park, California 91320

SAGE Publications India Pvt Ltd
C-236 Defence Colony
New Delhi 110 024

SAGE Publications Inc
275 South Beverly Drive
Beverly Hills, California 90212

British Library Cataloguing in Publication Data

Collins, Richard, *1946–*
    The economics of television: the U.K. case.
    —(Media culture and society).
    1. Television broadcasting—Economic aspects
    —Great Britain
    I. Title   II. Garnham, Nicholas
    III. Locksley, Gareth   IV. Series
    384.55'43'0941   HE8700.9.G7

    ISBN 0-8039-8112-0

Library of Congress catalog card number 87-062363

Printed in Great Britain by
J.W. Arrowsmith Ltd, Bristol

Contents

Preface   vi

1 The Peacock Committee and the
  Economic Analysis of Broadcasting   1

2 Production Costs in UK Television   20

3 The Internationalization of the Television
  Programme Market   50

4 The Finance of Broadcasting   98

5 The Peacock Report   111

References   129

Index   133

Preface

A Committee on Financing the British Broadcasting Corporation, known as the Peacock Committee after its chairman, Professor Alan Peacock, was established by the British Home Secretary in March 1985. Its brief was threefold. First, it was to assess the effects of the introduction of advertising or sponsorship on the BBC's broadcasting within the United Kingdom, either as an alternative or as a supplement to the income now received through the licence fee. This assessment was to include the financial and other consequences for the BBC, for independent television and independent local radio, for direct broadcasting satellites, for the press and the advertising industry and for the British Treasury. It was also to cover the impact on the range and quality of existing broadcasting services. Second, it was to identify a range of options for the introduction, in varying amounts and on different conditions, of advertising or sponsorship on some or all of the BBC's UK broadcasting, with an analysis of the advantages and disadvantages of each. Third, it was to consider any proposals for securing income from the consumer other than through the licence fee.

The research on which this book is based was commissioned by the Greater London Council in its final days. It was part of a wider research effort in support of the Council's interventions in the national debate about the future of broadcasting and about communications policy more generally which formed the background to the creation and work of the Peacock Committee. These interventions included the holding of public inquiries on the impact of cable television at a time when the government was introducing its cable legislation, and research on community radio and on the privatization of British Telecom. It also established a 'cultural industries' section of the Greater London Enterprise Board which supported alternative publishers and record and video distributors.

Our economic research was paralleled by the research of the Broadcasting Research Unit on audience perceptions and by the work of the Campaign for Press and Broadcasting Freedom to alert the broadcasting trade unions to the issues.

The debate about the future of broadcasting is shared with all western European countries (and, to some degree, with the United States and Canada). It is concerned in particular with the future of public service broadcasting in the face of competition from new cable and satellite services in what have been up to now protected national markets. Faced by the need to control public expenditure, governments, and the United Kingdom is no exception, have been increasingly unwilling to provide adequate licence-fee finance and have been tempted to turn to advertising to fill the gap.

A major issue in broadcasting economics — the availability of advertising finance and the impact of advertising finance on public service broadcasting — is not given sustained attention in this book. We recommend to readers the discussion of advertising finance in the Peacock report where the issue is thoroughly and perceptively treated. It would be otiose to summarize the Peacock Committee's conclusions on advertising, but two salient points are worth mentioning. The committee recognized that advertising finance is not likely to produce a programme mix that corresponds to viewers' preferences, and that the pool of advertising finance in the United Kingdom is insufficient to sustain the present broadcasting structure, that is, licence fees or other non-advertising revenue is required.

These are important conclusions which should bear on future discussion of broadcasting policy and, in particular, on that invited by the publication of the government's Green Paper on radio — *Radio: Choices and Opportunities* (Home Office, 1987) — which looked to advertising to finance additional British radio services.

However, this book's purpose is to address three different, though equally pertinent, questions. First, what is the nature of the television market? Second, what is happening to broadcasting costs and why? And third, what is the United Kingdom's position in the internationalization of television and, specifically, its role in the international trade in television programmes?

Although *The Economics of Television* is concerned with a particular period of time, and although it was occasioned by a specific commission itself inspired by a particular government initiative, we believe it has a number of enduring claims on the attention of the reader. The broadcasting environment is rapidly changing under the influence of new distribution technologies (notably satellites which are accelerating the internationalization of television) and new ideologies (the challenge of the market and consumer sovereignty to public service authority). Yet many of the forces perceived as new have a long-standing presence in the British television structure and many of the characteristics of the present order will survive. In the long term, we believe our discussion of the nature of the broadcasting market and the economic characteristics of information will remain of interest.

Particularly important features are the imperfectly competitive character of the broadcasting market, which requires some political system of allocations (best realized, in our view, by a public presence in the market, though not necessarily that which now exists); the outstanding cheapness of terrestrial broadcasting compared with other systems of distributing television; and the particular economic characteristics of the television programme and other information commodities.

Some parts of the book are specific, and are unavoidably tied to data that will be supplanted. The sections on the television programme trade and on the EEC Commission's publication, *Television Without Frontiers* (Commission of the European Communities, 1984), discuss matters that are changing literally day by day. However, certain long-term trends are evident even in these areas of concern, and we believe that, although the structures and conditions we describe are in flux as new policies are promulgated, the internationalization of broadcasting, already firmly established, will continue. The importance of the costs of television production, the modes of financing television and the UK's import and export trade in television programmes will remain. In these sections of the book we hope we have reconciled the need to present the findings of empirical studies (often introducing material into the public domain for the first time) with an analysis of the forces and structures that have had, and will continue to have, a major affect on British television. And it goes without saying that the importance of costs, finance and international trade is not confined to the United Kingdom.

We end with a discussion of the *Report of the Committee on Financing the BBC* — the Peacock report — which has obvious claims to attention in this book. It has occasioned a wide-ranging debate on broadcasting policy and a new government agenda. It contains invaluable information and analysis, especially on the broadcasting advertising market. And for a committee established by the government, it articulates an unprecedentedly radical view of the broadcasting authorities and the role of the consumer.

We wish to thank those whose work and co-operation have made this book possible. We are very grateful to the researchers and secretary of the Centre for Communication and Information Studies at the Polytechnic of Central London. Florabel Campbell-Atkinson, Philip Hayward and Daniel Re'em helped with research and production work and our debt to Jonathan Davis, the senior researcher is particularly large. We are also indebted to those broadcasters, regulators and producers who gave generously of their time and expertise. Our thanks to them.

CHAPTER ONE

The Peacock Committee and the Economic Analysis of Broadcasting

> Insofar as individuals in society have any objectives — be they social,
> political or economic — that are achievable via economic adjustments,
> then economists are best equipped to analyze the institutional implica-
> tions, albeit within a suitably formulated welfare economic framework.
> (Rowley and Peacock, 1975)

The broadcasting sector in the UK has more 'customers' than British
Telecom, or the Gas and Electricity Boards. No other sector can match
the time each day its customers consciously devote to the consumption
of its product. There are something like 49,000 people employed in
London alone in TV, film, video and cinema (Greater London
Council, 1985), while, in the whole of Britain there are only about
40,000 people employed in the manufacture of electronic computers
(*Business Monitor*, 1982: PQ 366). The 1982/83 London turnover of the
TV, film, video and cinema sector was just over £1 billion (see
Blanchard in Greater London Council, 1985) and the total output of
the broadly defined UK information technology sector was about
£3.25 billion (NEDO, 1984). Unlike many other industries, Britain's
broadcasters continue to produce at a quality that places them among
the best in the world. For example, by 1984 they had won in total
twenty-six Prix Italia more than France, West Germany, the USA and
Japan, our major industrial competitors, had collected between them.
Broadcasting is clearly a great industry in Britain, but whereas the
heating, ventilation, air conditioning and refrigeration sector has its
own economic development committee with the National Economic
Development Office (NEDO), broadcasting cannot even boast a
standard industrial classification!

The setting up of the Peacock Committee, the evidence that its
inquiry has elicited, and the debate on the future funding of UK
broadcasting that it has sparked off, have performed the valuable
function of placing the economics of broadcasting firmly at the centre
of the policy-making agenda. In a period of far-reaching and rapid
change in the broadcasting field, both nationally and internationally, it
may be true that the committee's terms of reference have been too

narrowly drawn, but it is a mistake, in our view, to criticize them on the grounds that they focus too narrowly on economic questions to the exclusion of more important cultural ones. On the contrary, such an economic focus should serve as a healthy antidote to that bias in favour of cultural questions divorced from economic ones, which was established by previous committees of inquiry, in particular the most recent under Lord Annan. The culturalist bias of that committee led to its failure to undertake any serious analysis of the economics of the UK broadcasting industry and its position in an increasingly international market. This meant that its recommendations were seriously flawed and it has proved a poor guide to future policy. The one concrete structural change that did result from its work, Channel Four, was set up on a different economic basis to that recommended, and continues to be an economically ill-understood part of the UK broadcasting system.

The culturalist bias of the Annan Committee is widely shared by broadcasters themselves and by those members of the cultural elite who see it as their business to keep broadcasting policy free of what they see as the philistine influence of economic analysis. But all cultural production and consumption rests upon and is, to a significant extent, determined by the allocation and utilization of scarce resources, and it is to that process of resource allocation that the craft of economics addresses itself.

Values and the Allocation of Resources

Before we examine what economics can tell us about broadcasting and the problems it faces, it is important to stress that economists, including Professor Peacock, rest their analyses upon a set of prior value assumptions. These values determine both the way in which problems are identified and the natue of their attempted solution. To take one example, the school that has dominated what economic analysis there has been of broadcasting is Paretian welfare economics.[1] That school bases its definition of the best or optimal social welfare on the outcome of individual, autonomous economic decisions expressible in terms of price. Such a definitional assumption takes for granted the existing distribution of income and property rights. It is reluctant to consider group decisions on welfare and interpersonal welfare comparisons. It also assumes the homogeneity of commodities, the perfect divisibility of both commodities and factors of production, and that all production functions are continuous.[2] Paretians end up with a static economy with no uncertainty about the future and perfect knowledge of the present. These conditions are met in perfect competition. Such a model of optimal resource allocation under market conditions is highly abstract and unrealistic. As Professor Peacock has written:

> Since perfect competition not only does not but indeed cannot exist as a universal phenomenon in the modern, advanced economy, the policy relevance of the Paretian approach, save under conditions of socialism, cannot be considered extensive. It should be remembered that any divergence of price from marginal cost (as occurs within the large-group monopolistic competition case) debars attainment of a Paretian optimum.
>
> Too often, the point is ignored by Paretian welfare economists who proceed from the rigorous formal analysis of the Paretian model to casual if not careless policy discussion in which the word 'perfect' is dropped (by accident or by design) and competition, of whatever kind, is treated (incorrectly) as a sufficient welfare-maximizing mechanism. (Rowley and Peacock, 1975: 25)

However, Professor Peacock's own liberal alternative welfare economics rests upon equally arbitrary value assumptions. Peacock has been at pains to stress that, in the real world, optimality is a case of finding the least worst solution derived from a concrete analy$\ldots$ of real markets, real institutional arrangements and real human behaviour rather than using any notion of 'perfect' competition as a measure. Paretians argue that in cases of market imperfection (a deviation from the perfect benchmark) such as monopoly, the state has a positive duty to intervene through regulations. But Peacock takes the view that individual freedom rather than optimized material welfare is the primary goal of policy and thus any intervention by the state and any form of coercion is viewed with a priori suspicion. This is crucial for broadcasting economics and policy for two reasons. Firstly because such a position will focus on the coercive nature of the licence fee rather than on its efficiency as a resource allocating mechanism, and secondly because, in Peacock's own words, 'liberals prefer even private monopoly to public monopoly, where a competitive solution does not seem possible' (Rowley and Peacock, 1975: 115).

Even if we wished to resist the definition of the social good in economic terms, we need to understand economic forces if we are to control them. UK broadcasting exists, whether we like it or not, in a market economy not only on a national level, but also, and increasingly, on an international level. We may for good policy reasons wish the government to insulate UK broadcasting from the forces of that international market if it were possible. But in order to do so we need to start by understanding them. What questions then does economics pose of a broadcasting system?

Economics is not merely descriptive. It deals with the allocation not just of resources, but of scarce resources. Thus it is centrally concerned with how allocative decisions are made, their efficiency and their social impact. The question of allocative efficiency is posed at three levels: the first concerns the distribution of resources between competing sectors. The question is how much expenditure in aggregate should go to broadcasting as opposed to any other sector. At this macro level an optimal allocation between sectors is achieved when no further redistribution between the sectors could raise the total welfare of society. Following the macro allocation to broadcasting and other sectors, the other two issues relate to a slightly different concept of efficiency. The first centres on the internal efficiency of the 'firm' and the way in which it uses its resources to maximize its output for the level of inputs. In terms of broadcasting this would involve minimizing the cos.s of programme production for a given type, quality and length of programme. But mere production efficiency is not enough. The third issue of optimal allocation involves the ability of consumers to direct producers to provide the goods they require in the right quantities, qualities, prices ranges and places, given the state of technology. The requirements of consumers are termed 'final demand' and an optimal allocation is achieved when these are satisfied by least-cost solutions and in such a way that consumers are not exploited by the 'excess' profits of producers. This means prices must reflect costs. Underpinning these issues is the ability of the sovereign consumer to direct resources to their preferred goods and services which are produced in the most technically efficient manner. The relevance of consumer sovereignty to broadcasting is the ability of viewers to guide TV producers to provide the programmes they want in the bundles they want and at a price close to their costs.

The three levels of efficiency interact, since we are dealing with a continuous process not a static structure. That is to say, in market economies, it is the pattern of final demand that largely determines macro-resource allocation to particular activities and their productive efficiency. There is constant interaction, whether through competitive markets or planning mechanisms of a more or less political nature, between supply and demand, each mutually determining the other.

These questions of allocative efficiency are being asked of the UK broadcasting system at a time when the existing market structure is under pressure from two related directions. Firstly, new technologies of distribution — cable, satellite and video-cassette recorders (VCRs)

— are becoming available which provide a potential for significant market restructuring. Cable and the use by satellites of higher frequencies are lowering the barriers to entry raised by spectrum scarcity, and satellites are providing the means for extensive transnational TV broadcasting. Secondly, the rising real costs of broadcasting (i.e. adjusted for inflation) are increasing the financial pressures on broadcasters to broaden their market base. VCRs are altering the nature of the broadcasting commodity and the pattern of consumption by placing control over the time of consumption in the hands of the viewer rather than the scheduler.

The Economics of Broadcasting Production

Because of the Peacock Committee's terms of reference most of the recent debate on the economics of UK broadcasting has focused on problems of funding or the overall allocation of resources. One line of research has focused on the desirability as allocative mechanisms of the different available sources of finance for broadcasting — licence, government grant, advertising or Pay TV — and on the differential impact on other broadcasting sectors and on other media if the BBC was to be financed out of advertising revenue. Important as these questions are, we believe that they can only be adequately analysed if we first understand the nature of broadcasting as a specific system of production, which itself can only be understood if we understand the nature of the broadcasting commodity which it produces.

In analysing the economics of broadcasting it helps to place broadcasting within the wider context of cultural production, distribution and consumption in general. This sphere of social production and the cultural industries which now dominate it (book, magazine and newspaper publishing, the music and film industries as well as broadcasting) share certain economic characteristics with the consumer goods sector in general, but they also share certain specific and unusual economic characteristics of their own. These might be termed the microeconomics of broadcasting and are the subject of the first part of this chapter.

An analysis of the characteristics identified can help us to understand the economic problems of UK broadcasting in three ways. First, it can help us to understand what is specific to broadcasting itself and differentiates it from the other cultural industries. Second, as the media's functions and products merge, under combined economic and technological pressures, into a common set of multi-media products, services and institutions (films circulating through cinemas, Pay TV, broadcast TV and video-cassettes as successful segments of a unified market or records merging with pop-videos, etc.),[3] an understanding of the total macroeconomic context can help us to see the economic options facing broadcasting and its potential lines of development. Third, a knowledge of the economics of the cultural field at a macro level can help in analysing from the point of view of industrial policy the models of intervention and the rule changes that may follow from the Peacock inquiry. For example, some members of the Peacock Committee appear charmed by the Peter Jay thesis (Peacock, 1986a: 112–18). This contrasts unfavourably the current state of broadcasting in the UK with a highly misleading and idealized image of the world of print publishing as a realm of unproblematic competitive freedom. This is because Jay does not have a realistic understanding of the microeconomics of the cultural industries which leads him to advocate policies with adverse macroeconomic consequences. The second part of this chapter deals with the macroeconomic issues of broadcasting.

Economic Characteristics of the Commodity

We define the broadcasting commodity as the total set of broadcasting output which results from the interaction between the set of audience needs which broadcasting attempts to satisfy and the historically given set of productive resources which the broadcasting industry has at its disposal for the fulfilment of that task. It may seem at first glance that there is an obvious answer to the question, what is the broadcasting commodity? It is a TV or radio programme. But, as we shall see, it can as cogently be argued that the appropriate unit of analysis is the programme segment, especially that segment between two successive commercial breaks, or the channel, or the total broadcasting service. The definition of the broadcasting commodity will vary as between the broadcaster, the programme maker and the viewer. An independent producer may see an individual programme as the commodity while a broadcasting organization may define the commodity as the totality of scheduling over a season and beyond.

Earlier we stated that broadcasting is a 'peculiar' economic activity. It is the peculiar characteristics of broadcasting which make economic analysis of the sector so difficult. The peculiarities also lead to forms of government intervention that are not commonly encountered in other fields of economic activity. The whole sector is subject to extensive regulation over its structure, ownership, finance, content, behaviour and performance. This regulation is both national and international. Further, the form competition takes in the sector is highly unusual because the basic mode of competition — by price — is virtually non-existent. These peculiarities follow directly from the nature of the commodity itself. It is to this that we now turn.

Immateriality and Novelty

The broadcasting commodity shares certain economic characteristics with other cultural goods, such as a film, a newspaper or a record, which stem first from the fact that the essential quality from which their use-value derives is immaterial — it is in one form or another symbolic meaning which is merely carried by a material carrier such as celluloid, vinyl, or the waves of the radio spectrum and a cathode ray tube. It is the message not the medium that provides value to the user and the message is immaterial or intangible.

Then there is the question of the essence of the meaning production from which we derive the value of such cultural transactions. If we already have information we do not need it again; new value can only be derived from a new, novel product. This is not true of material goods, such as a loaf of bread or a washing machine, whose value can only be extracted by a process of material consumption, a process which can be indefinitely repeated so long as the need persists. We seek to repeat the consumption of essentially the same loaf of bread and the washing machine provides a long stream of services. A number of key economic characteristics of the cultural commodity and of the production process designed to produce them derive from these characteristics.

A Public Good

Because a cultural good is immaterial it is not destroyed by the act of consumption. If I watch a TV programme it in no way diminishes anyone else's chance of watching it. It thus possesses one of the key characteristics of a public good.[4] Private goods are rationed between consumers by prices. The number of loaves a household consumes is limited by its disposable income in relation to its need and the price of bread. Loaves are distributed between families in this way because there is a scarcity — i.e. not limitless supply — of the ingredients of bread. Once a household consumes a loaf it is no longer available to anyone else. It is 'rival' in consumption. The price system is our society's method of allocating under scarcity. But broadcast material does not conform to the characteristics of private goods.

Broadcast TV programmes are technically 'non-rival' in the way we have described. They are also 'non-excludable', for when a programme is broadcast to one household it is simultaneously broadcast for all those households with TVs in the reception area — this is, after all, the meaning of broadcasting. Technologically it is now possible to exclude viewers by scrambling signals. But what would be the point? Exclusion only has a purpose if it is combined with the price mechanism. Exclusion through technological devices would only be worthwhile if the expected revenues exceeded the costs of exclusion.

These two conditions, non-rival and non-excludable, cause the price system of allocation through the market to fail. A private entrepreneur looking to sell broadcasting to viewers would find it extremely difficult to recover expenditures and would be unlikely to make them in the first instance. Governments tend to intervene where markets fail. Under Paretian assumptions, governments will tend to replace the market by some form of public provision and appropriate public finance. But the Liberal perspective would lead the government to enhance the market — to find some way of making it work by, for example, making exclusion feasible. This implies private finance of the service.

The public-good characteristic of broadcasting is reinforced by the low to zero extra cost of reaching an extra viewer — the 'marginal cost' to the producer of additional viewers. Since prices charged to consumers should reflect costs incurred by the producer (for the maximization of welfare) and to avoid consumer 'exploitation', it follows that any price charged should be zero or near zero even if exclusion were possible.

Near-zero marginal costs can characterize many cultural commodities, for example, the costs of making an extra copy of a record or tape are virtually zero, the cost difference between a hardback and paperback book is about 50p and on long print runs paperbacks can be made for 10p. All consumer goods industries are systems for exploiting economies of scale. When a large number of copies of an original prototype is reproduced the unit (average) cost of each copy falls. This can generate a growth cycle when falling costs are reflected in lower prices which expand the market, facilitating further copies and another drop in the unit cost of each copy, and so on. This process is carried to its ultimate in the cultural industries where very cheap and highly efficient technologies of reproduction are used to reproduce the product. Consequently, the cost of providing the commodity to additional members of an audience — the cost of reproduction — is very low in absolute terms. But it is also extremely low in relation both to the cost of the original prototype and to the value the potential reader, viewer or listener attributes to that product. Broadcasting represents the ultimate development of this trend because the process of reproduction is instantaneous (the time it takes for a radio signal to pass from transmitter to reception set), and the marginal cost of each extra viewer or listener in a given reception area is zero to the producer (it isn't, of course, zero for the consumer since it requires some investment, however small, in reception). Thus the potential returns for economies of scale are virtually continuous, which creates heavy pressure to constantly expand audience share to the point of monopoly saturation.

R and D and Innovation

Clearly broadcasting and cultural commodities are very different from those in other sectors of the economy because of their rapidly declining costs (which have important implications for the pricing of products and the financing of the sector), and the non-destructive nature of the act of consumption. If the cultural commodity were a normal consumer good, these characteristics would lead rapidly to stagnation since product life is virtually eternal. With normal commodities, even in the absence of product innovation, the economic cycle of production and consumption is kept going by the need constantly to repeat the same act of consumption. But this is where the fact of constant novelty comes in. The need for product innovation is not of course unique to the cultural industries. It is indeed central to consumer industries as a competitive strategy. But only in the cultural industries is extremely rapid product innovation a central condition of existence. The result of this is that what is referred to in the cultural industries and in broadcasting as production should more properly in comparative terms be described as research and development. Each book, each issue of a newspaper or magazine, each recording, each TV or radio programme, is a prototype. What in a normal consumer-goods industry would be regarded as production is, in fact, in the cultural industries, a process of reproduction. As we have seen in broadcasting, this is instantaneous which is why it so easily escapes the attention that is its due. Because a high proportion of the production costs of the cultural industries are necessarily devoted to R and D, each new production involves the launching of a new product on the market for which the demand is necessarily very uncertain. Moreover, because of the demand for novelty, its product life tends to be very short (the shelf life of the typical top-selling paperback or record can be measured in weeks and major films are made or broken in the first few weeks of their release). Thus each individual product is a very high-risk investment, as many film investors have found to their cost. Furthermore, because of the immateriality of the cultural commodity and its resulting public-good characteristics, there is a tendency for it to be difficult to realize value; pirated copies can easily be made and distributed and, in spite of the drive towards novelty, there is also the countervailing possibility of easy repetition and reconsumption. Books can be reread and records constantly replayed.

Normal private goods are easily rationed by prices, their consumption by one person precludes the same consumption by another, and their costs do not continuously fall to zero. In these conditions value and profit can be realized by the supplier of private goods. We have an understanding of how this private economy works, how the actors behave and can anticipate responses to any particular stimulus. But these conditions do not hold for the cultural industries and it would be inappropriate to map the model of the private commodity straight on to that of the cultural industries. The characteristics discussed above have elicited different modes of operation and production from those followed in the traditional private consumer-goods sector.

Structural Implications

There are at least three sets of actors in the broadcasting sector — those who make programmes (products), those who compile programmes into channels (catalogue) and those who distribute the channels. Often these different functions are performed within one organization, but this is not always the case. The distinctions have been disguised in the UK because, in the BBC, all three functions have been contained within one organization, and because, between the IBA (responsible for transmission) and ITV (responsible for production and schedule construction), there exists a very close interrelationship. The Channel Four model has further disaggregated these functions. The relationship between the three sets of actors and other external markets, including the final consumer, determines the structure of the sector. The special characteristics of broadcasting, and of the cultural industries in general, have implications for the structure of the sectors and their modes of operation. Historically the cultural industries have adopted a number of strategies to deal with the peculiarities of their products and the problems they raise in the context of markets. Together all these factors determine the structure of the sector as it exists.

Ranges and Flows

The first set of strategies adopted by the cultural industries has involved the exploitation not only of economies of scale but also of economies of scope. By controlling a range of products the chances of making a hit with consumer taste is increased. Th revenue from that hit bears no relation to the production cost of the individual commodity and profits can be realized on a programme of production. Miege et al. (1986) have identified two distinct ways of achieving this end, one being the editorial style of production, that is, the ability to put together a range of different distinct products into a list, or catalogue, which can be marketed as a whole. The other is what they call the 'culture de flot' (flow culture), of which newspapers and broadcasting are the classic cases. Here, a range of items appealing to a range of possible needs and tastes is assembled into a constantly renewed stream which is sold to consumers as a whole. Consumers pay for the service so long as a high enough proportion of the content is to their taste. It is in this sense that each broadcasting programme can be more properly seen as a story or feature in a newspaper or magazine, and the commodity being offered is the total schedule, whether over one channel or several. From the point of view of economic strategies the crucial matter is the range of material over which central editorial and financial control is exercised. This is a crucial point for current debates about broadcasting, for it is often assumed that cross-subsidization between programme types and channels is a feature of public service broadcasting. It is not. However, it is a general feature of the cultural industries under competitive market conditions and is a condition of their survival. This distinction depends on the extent to which cross-subsidization can be exercised and on whether it is directed towards a greater range of choice or increased profitability.

Clearly, any restriction on the range of programmes (products) that a broadcaster can offer will damage the channel's viability, for this is to restrict the choice-set from which a portfolio can be constructed. In these circumstances the opportunities for balancing 'losses' by 'profits' become increasingly limited. And this is as true of audience figures (the broadcaster's 'reach') as it is of direct financial returns. Thus if the BBC were to be confined to a narrowly defined 'public service' ghetto, it would be forced to become increasingly cautious in its programming policy, even within that restrictive range, and consumer choice would be severely restricted.

This ability to control a portfolio of programming should not be confused with the question of the choice between mixed-programming and specialized channels for the preferred scheduling type. Those who, like Peter Jay, argue for the consumer advantages of multi-channel broadcasting, often work, if only tacitly, with the model of a highly segmented market in which a range of distinct, individual, specialist channels constantly compete with one another for the viewers' custom. Often the magazine market is used as the model at which to aim. In fact, of course, while it may be possible for a channel (or an individual magazine) to survive in certain 'niche' markets, in general a publishing house or media company designs its products to cover a range of market segments. It is significant that cable offers bundles and tiers of channels rather than a single channel, and that specialist channel providers, such as HBO (Home Box Office, a US movie channel), are being pushed towards the network programming model so as not to be confined to a narrow, uneconomic audience segment. It should further be noted that it is the magazine wholesalers and retailers, not the publishers, with whom the broadcasting services should more properly be compared, and that this is a sector characterized by a high degree of concentration.

Distribution
Both the editorial and flow strategies require some control over access to an audience on a regular basis if economies of scope are to be realized. Thus it is control over distribution, not production in its narrow sense, that is crucial both in print, publishing, film, records and broadcasting. Broadcasting represents, technically and thus organizationally, the ultimate development of that logic, symbolized by and realized in control over access to the transmitter. So long as such distributional control is realized, relations to production proper can be organized in a number of ways. These range from a highly fragmented system of contracting-out and buying-in from production houses or even, as in book publishing, individual 'creative' workers, to centralized large-scale production on semi-industrial lines with significant proportions of permanently-employed salaried and waged workers, as with the BBC model. In all these cases the distributor will attempt to exercise as much detailed control over the nature and content of the individual product as is attainable. This is the function of 'editors' even when they are dealing with individual creative workers like authors. The notion that independent producers can make any product for the distributor is not feasible from the perspective of the distributor. In fact independents are producing 'to order' and their 'independence' refers to their ownership status rather than their product. For the flow-culture solution to the problem of providing a range of items appealing to a range of viewers' needs, the centralized

BBC-type model is frequently more rational and more efficient. In these circumstances a constant production flow closely allied to large-scale distribution systems is advantageous. However, as the US network system shows, it is by no means essential.

The Time Barrier

Flow culture is in a powerful position, and was created to that end — to exploit the time element of cultural value. One way of avoiding the piracy problem and thus retaining control over the realization of the value of the commodity, while at the same time exploiting to the full the value of novelty, is to accelerate the product cycle, both creating the need for constant reconsumption and leaving no time for others to exploit the same market unless they too have access to an equally rapid distribution system. Again broadcasting is the ultimate development of this logic. But clearly such a logic applies less to some categories of programming than others. News and live sport are highly time-dependent, while much fictional TV is not. Indeed, in the latter area, there is the increasing growth of a secondary market in repeats and home videos.[5]

The time-dependency of the broadcasting commodity is extremely important in relation both to the structure of the industry and to competition within the industry. Welfare economists base their arguments upon a concept of the commodity as divisible and substitutable. But to the extent that a broadcast programme is time-dependent, the act of broadcasting is neither. It is for this reason that peak-time is peak-time. Part of the utility offered is the ability to watch the programme at the time you want to. However, only in a pay-per-view system is it possible to ration a favourable time slot by price. In all other systems competition tends to discriminate against minority audiences, not only in terms of the programmes produced, but also in terms of their time of showing. Clearly this important characteristic of the broadcasting commodity has been significantly changed by the introduction of VCR-based time-shift recording, but only for those types of programming that are closely time-dependent, and even then at a cost. The convenience of not having to time-shift is worth something.

Organization and Control

It is likely therefore, under conditions of increased channel capacity and increased competition between media sources and for limited audience time, that the mode of production for the two types of output will diverge somewhat, with certain types of audio-visual material increasingly passing into the editorial mode with a characteristically more fragmented, freelance production organization, while the classic centralized TV mode is retained for news and sport. This trend, however, should not be exaggerated since there is demonstrably a value to consumers in reducing search-time, and in competitive conditions they would appear to be loyal to channels that can provide quality control over a programming range. Certainly HBO has been dragged back towards the classic, mixed-programming, network model in order to maximize its market share. Similarly the US networks have always retained direct control over news and in many cases sports, sub-contracting only entertainment programming to external producers. Thus, within what is called broadcasting, we can observe two different organizational logics which are likely to develop in different ways. Which organizational model is chosen will depend, under competitive conditions, upon existing institutional cultures — all production systems exhibit high degrees of inertia — and also on the relative returns in different instances to economies of scale and economies of specialization. An organization as big as the BBC is, in general, in a position to exploit both, since its output is big enough to retain specialized teams across a range of programme types. On the other hand it has the potential for substantial diseconomies and is likely to operate under conditions of organizational slack (or x-inefficiency).

Non-Price Competition

Market economies are traditionally viewed as systems where firms compete with prices (for a given quality of product) for customers. Further, the process of competition forces prices to reflect costs of production and for these to reflect efficient modes of production. Competition therefore performs the function of keeping both prices and costs down to take advantage of technological developments and economies available to the enterprise. In turn this implies internal efficiency for the firm (called x-efficiency). However, a large proportion of the economics literature is concerned with those modes of operation where these conditions do not obtain (see Cyert and March, 1963). Price competition is frequently suspended because firms realize that is the most damaging form of competition or because they are insulated from market forces by a monopoly position or regulations concerning entry. A large body of economics is devoted to x-inefficiency — the case where firms are not producing at the least cost — and to the organizational and market consequences of this state of affairs.[6] In such circumstances the link between prices and costs, and the downward pressure on both, is loose. This is not to say that firms do not compete — they compete in different ways. The product itself becomes the weapon, with variations in quality, design, style, colour, packaging, technical standards and services rendered taking over from price as instruments for gaining customers. These constant changes are supported by advertising and other promotional expenditure, as well as by R and D to support product development. Of course, all of these activities are expensive, so that non-price competition implies an upward pressure on costs which can only be offset by technological advance.

Non-price competition is prevalent throughout the cultural industries, but is especially powerful in broadcasting for two reasons: because there is no direct price relationship between production and either the size or intensity of audience demand; and because unit costs of consumption are so low that, even without the technology for Pay TV, it is difficult, if not impossible, to create effective price discrimination between individual programmes. This centrality of non-price competition in broadcasting has a profound influence on the structure and costs of production.

Costs

In the motor industry, a firm can plan to produce a car with a given number of performance characteristics (e.g. acceleration, load capacity, fuel consumption) which are related to known consumer demand. Then production can be planned so that the product is designed down to a target price. Depending on the sensitivity of buyers to prices charged, a number of price/quality strategies (e.g. L, GL, GLX) can then be adopted. Such an approach is impossible in the cultural sector for several reasons. Firstly, demand is very uncertain. For example, the number of cultural products that flop far exceeds the number of motor car marques that fail. Further there is a de-linkage of costs of production with the value of the product, whereas with motor cars costs of production reflect the 'quality' attributes of the car. These characteristics are exaggerated in broadcasting because of two factors previously described. The first is the very low unit costs of consumption. As Ehrenberg and Barwise (1982: 4–8) have calculated, the cost of UK broadcasting to the consumer is 1.5p per hour for ITV and 2p per hour for BBC. The second factor is that the act of consumption (except in the case of Pay TV) is not accompanied by the direct act of payment. But it is also noticeable in other cultural subsectors that products are offered within broadly-fixed price categories which are not related to the nature of a specific product in that range. For instance, the prices for a given cinema do not in general alter from film to film, and the same is true for books, records, magazines and newspapers. This prevalence of non-price competition has two effects: by raising barriers to entry it further reinforces the tendencies to monopoly control that stem from economies of scale and scope and, even in competitive conditions, it places upward pressure on production costs.

Such upward pressures have been reinforced in British TV by buoyant advertising revenue and the fact, as Harry Henry has pointed out in evidence to the Peacock inquiry (ITCA, 1985), that the amount of advertising available and its price determines neither the amount nor the costs of production. Upward cost pressures have been further exacerbated by the structure of the levy. The levy is raised by the IBA on behalf of the Treasury as a percentage on profits. It is designed to ensure a return to the public purse from the monopoly exploitation of a public resource — the radio spectrum. However, its structure has encouraged the padding of production expenses (see National Audit Office, 1985; Home Office, 1986). The amount of revenue merely places a ceiling on production costs. Certainly in the BBC, production costs will rise to match available income, since there is no incentive to control them. Further, because of non-price competition, peer-group rivalry and an ideology of creativity there is an in-built cost-inflation dynamic. But it should not be thought that the introduction of competition will mitigate these effects. Indeed, to the contrary, in the competitive, profit-oriented system in the United States, the index of costs per programme hour rose, in cash terms, from 100, in 1964, to 242.9 in 1976, according to figures published by the Baumols (1976). This feature of the US broadcasting system is illustrated in Table 1.1. It should also be noted that cost inflation is also prevalent in the press and film industries.

Cost Inflation

Further cost-inflation pressures stem from the incidence of Baumol's disease. His analysis of US data, not only in the traditional performing arts, but also in the film and network TV industries, leads him to characterize such industries as ones of continual decline to stagnation (see Baumol and Bowen, 1966; Baumol et al., 1984). What Baumol argues is that the basic commodity-production process of the cultural industries is inherently labour intensive because it is concerned with constantly producing prototypes. In other industries there have been technological advances bringing about productivity gains which lower the production costs of output. But the technology of Shakespeare's *Othello* has been unchanged for over 400 years. The real level of wages

Table 1.1 *Cost per TV Programme Hour for US Television,*
1964/65 to 1976/77

Season	Cost per Programme Hour (in US dollars)	Programme Index
1964	126	100.0
1965	136	107.9
1966	156	123.8
1967	176	139.7
1968	181	143.7
1969	188	149.2
1970	195	154.8
1971	200	158.7
1972	208	165.1
1973	204	161.9
1974	213	169.0
1975	252	200.0
1976	306	242.9

Based on data in *Television* and *Broadcasting* magazines. The data are average costs for the three networks (ABC, CBS and NBC) per programme hour, all evening entertainment series, and exclude feature films, sports and news programmes.

Source: Charles River Associates cited in Baumol and Baumol (1976: 113).

is determined by the overall level of productivity in the economy which has been rising for centuries. Since wages in, say, the theatre are linked to overall real wages, over time the theatre becomes a more expensive activity relative to any other activity where productivity has advanced, though film and broadcasting have raised the productivity of an individual performance of *Othello*. Nevertheless the possibilities of exploiting the productivity gains from capital investment in labour-saving technology in the production of a TV programme is strictly limited. Indeed, as the BBC argued to Peat, Marwick (1985), much capital investment is a form of non-price competition which increases costs rather than being labour-saving. Given this unbalanced application of productivity-enhancing advances in technology, there is an inexorable tendency for the real costs of cultural production to rise relative to those industries that experience technological innovations that raise productivity (i.e. consume less resources per unit of output produced). This is not to say that there have been no productivity gains in the entire broadcasting system. For example, the taping of programmes that were previously shown live and had a momentary existence has extended their life indefinitely. There have also been technological advances in the transmission of programmes, for example by satellite, so that larger audiences can be reached at a lower unit cost. It remains to be seen how much further productivity can be advanced in these segments of the broadcasting system, but in the field of the production of programmes Baumol's disease is already apparent.

Competitive Pressures and Cost Pressures

What are the structural effects of these upward pressures on costs in the cultural industries? Under competitive conditions at least, cultural entrepreneurs, for instance TV companies, will be forced to exploit economies of scale to the full in order to keep unit costs down in the face of these inflationary pressures on relative costs and prices. They can do this by expanding the market for their products, thereby facilitating economies of scale. However, the national market for which broadcasters are competing is strictly limited. The market for TV sets is now highly saturated and it is difficult to increase significantly the already high number of hours viewed per day. Thus, as the costs of production rise, so too must the unit costs of consumption. This trend is exaggerated as the number of competing channels rises and the audience for each channel so decreases. Three outcomes follow from these developments: (a) increasing competition for a given national broadcasting audience, (b) increasing international competition as national producers attempt to penetrate foreign markets, and (c) increased attempts to extend the product life by exploiting archives through repeats and syndication. All these moves, of course, are either mutually incompatible (because not every broadcaster can 'win') or they lead to diminished audience choice. The only alternative to a reduction of choice is to increase prices in one way or another and this leads us to the debate on financing that gave rise to the Peacock inquiry. It is for this reason that even without the introduction of competitive new technologies and expansion of distribution channels, broadcasting would be entering an era of more intensive competition in the absence of protective national regulation and increased funding from whatever source.

Consequences

Unless fifth generation computers and robots can wholly take over TV production, the incidence of Baumol's disease can only be postponed. In such a situation there will be constant pressure on labour costs from managers in the cultural sector generally[7] and in broadcasting in particular. Whether such pressures are, from the audience's point of view, dysfunctional is a matter of empirical investigation and judgement, but it is inherently difficult to determine because of the weak linkage between production cost and audience satisfaction. What is clear is that policy choices between the BBC production model, the ITV production model and the Channel Four model, from the point of view of productive efficiency, are of crucial significance, and thus that the relative costs of the various production systems and their determination is a matter of wide public importance. The determination of broadcasting production costs cannot be separated from the question of the appropriate position of national UK broadcasting in the international market and the level at which, for either cultural or employment reasons, the UK should sustain a national broadcasting presence. We therefore turn in the following sections to an analysis of production costs and of the trade in programmes, before returning to the question of how broadcasting should be financed.

Notes

1. See, for example, Winch (1971) for an exposition of the Paretian position.
2. Abstract technical assumptions are usually included in economic models. Perfectly divisible factors of production and commodities are those that can be hired and bought in whatever quantities required. This condition may hold for say electricity, but it becomes unrealistic in many other instances. For example, labour can be hired by the hour, but it is far more normal to have much longer contracts. Here an 'indivisibility' would appear. A production function shows the relationship between the inputs and outputs of an organization given the state of technology. If factors are perfectly divisible, any combination can be used in production and perfectly divisible levels of output can be achieved. In such circumstances the production function is continuous. However, for TV these assumptions are unrealistic. Output of TV programmes must conform to particular lengths and formats — e.g. a programme of exactly 50 minutes may be required, not a programme of 42 minutes.
3. Takeovers in the media industries have been a common feature of the recent scene with firms like News Corporation, BPCC and the troubled Cannon being prominent. At the same time the notion of a cross-media product has been introduced into films, TV series, videos, books, music and various related merchandise.
4. For a detailed discussion of the public-good concept see Houghton (1970), especially part two and the contributions of Samuelson.
5. For example: 'The retail value of pre-recorded video cassettes bought or (predominantly) hired in the UK during 1985 totalled nearly £400 million. The cinema box office grossed about £140 million.' Tim Pulleine, 'A-Grades Rock the Schlock', *The Guardian* (8 December 1986).
6. An excellent review of the issues involved can be found in Marris and Müller (1980).
7. These pressures have been behind the moves of publishers Rupert Murdoch and Eddie Shah to start up new, technology-based operations away from the traditional centres of printing.

CHAPTER TWO

Production Costs in UK Television

TV broadcasting's costs of production and their relation to the range and quality of TV broadcasting output are issues central to broadcasting policy precisely because, as our analysis shows, the broadcasting market is so imperfect and this imperfection is not subject to a technological fix. Thus competition is not available to policy-makers as a means of ensuring x-efficiency.

Moreover, it is the escalation of broadcasting costs and the pressure this puts on the level of the licence fee which, at a time of low economic growth and intense pressures to control levels of public expenditure, tempts governments of all political persuasions to try to depoliticize the issue by shifting the burden from licence fee to advertising and from the public to the private sector. For politicians, the overwhelming advantage of the market is that they can absolve themselves of the responsibility for the outcome it produces.

Thus the question of broadcasting costs was central to the work of the Peacock Committee. Their lack of success in dealing convincingly with the problem illustrates both its intractable nature and the difficulties of extracting adequate data from the broadcasters on which to base a serious analysis of the cost structure and dynamics of UK television industries. But it is significant that the only concrete policy initiatives to stem so far from the Peacock report are both attempts to control costs — namely the linking of the licence fee to the retail price index (RPI) and the proposed imposition on the BBC and ITV of a requirement to take an increasing proportion of their programmes, rising to 25 percent over four years, from the independent production sector.

The Licence Fee and the Cost Question

The BBC's most recent licence-fee claim was based upon a notion of 'broadcasting inflation' — the pressure on the licence-fee system stemming from the growing mismatch between the general level of price inflation and the apparently inexorable rate of growth of broadcasting production costs. This mismatch has been disguised in recent years by the high level of gearing incorporated within the licence-fee income by the rapid shift from monochrome to colour set-ownership, with its significantly higher licence fee. This gearing is now largely exhausted (see Table 2.1).

Table 2.1   *Ratios of Colour to Monochrome Licences, 1978 to 1986*

| | Number of Licences (thousands) | | Ratio | Change over Previous Year |
	Colour	Monochrome	(colour: mono)	(%)
1978	11,049	7100	1.6:1	+30
1979	12,131	6250	1.9:1	+19
1980	12,902	5383	2.4:1	+26
1981	13,780	4888	2.8:1	+17
1982	14,261	4294	3.3:1	+18
1983	14,699	3796	3.9:1	+18
1984	15,370	3261	4.7:1	+20
1985	15,820	2896	5.5:1	+17
1986	16,025	2679	6.0:1	+9

Source: BBC Annual Report and Handbook 1987.

But any licence-fee claim by the BBC, and the government's decision as to the level of the licence fee, are necessarily based upon an assessment of the costs of producing a given service. The licence fee is, in effect, a contract between the government, on behalf of the licence-fee payers, and the BBC to deliver a given service at a given price.

Prior to the Peacock report two possible means of taking political pressure off the licence fee were canvassed, either linking it to an agreed inflation index, or setting up a public utilities commission of some sort to set the licence fee. In both cases a publicly acceptable method of determining broadcasting costs and their rate of inflation would have been required. In the event, as we have seen, the government has chosen the easier option of pegging the licence to the RPI. But if TV production costs continue to rise faster than the RPI, thus putting the BBC's ability to meet its public-service programming objectives under increasing pressure, while at the same time the gap between the BBC's and ITV's incomes continues to grow, this arrangement is likely to come under increasing political pressure. Indeed the government has already commissioned a study of the feasibility and effects of moving the BBC's funding onto a subscription basis in an attempt to see how far the problem can be avoided by phasing out the licence fee altogether.

The IBA, ITV and the Cost Question

The IBA, both in judging between franchise applicants and in enforcing the terms of franchises, has to be able to make judgements on the effects on the financial health of an ITV company of imposing a given set of programme requirements. In the case of Channel Four it has to decide the appropriate level of the ITV companies' subscription, which is in its turn based upon a judgement as to the costs of producing Channel Four's schedule.

Judgements on the structure and appropriate level of additional payments by the ITV companies (the levy), both by government and the IBA, are also based upon assessments of cost. On the urging of the IBA in 1974, the levy was changed from a percentage of net advertising revenue to a percentage of profits, on the grounds that the previous system produced a conflict between programme production investment, on the one hand, and profits, on the other, to the implied detriment of programme production. However, the system that replaced it almost certainly contributed to cost inflation by removing much of the incentive to control production costs and has indeed recently been changed for that very reason. The IBA now collects, on behalf of the Exchequer, a tax equalling 45 percent of profits on domestic operations (after deductions which included a 'free slice' of at least £800,000) and 25 percent of profits from the sales of programmes overseas. This new system will have to be monitored in its turn to assess its impact on costs and especially on the relation between domestic production costs and overseas sales.

Cost Comparisons

The comparison of production costs, both between different sectors of the TV industry in the UK and between the UK and other national systems of TV production, is important for three reasons:

1. In the absence of competition it can be used as one method of judging relative efficiency.

2. It can give us some indication of the likely impact of international competition between the TV production industries of different nations.

3. Because the claim that the independent sector has a lower cost structure than the BBC or ITV underpins the policy, recommended by the Peacock report and taken up by government, of establishing a quota for independent production on the BBC and ITV.

However, reliable and meaningful cost comparisons for UK TV production are extremely difficult. Those cost comparisons which have been carried out between BBC, ITV and the independent sector are extremely limited in scope and are unavailable for independent public scrutiny. The usefulness of such comparisons is limited by the following factors:

1. Overall costs are influenced more by the scheduling mix than by the production costs of individual programmes.

2. Even within a distinct programme category it is difficult to ensure that one is comparing like with like because of the potential range of differing production values even within that category.

3. Because of the potential economies of scale and scope in broadcasting, one-off comparisons between programmes are highly misleading.

4. The structure of the different sectors and the system-costs imposed by regulatory requirements differ between sectors. For instance, the BBC is centralized while ITV is a regionally based, federal system. Cost structures differ between organizations based on a high percentage of permanently employed staff and in-house production resources, such as the BBC, on the one hand, and those based upon freelance labour and hired facilities, such as the independent sector. The independent sector does not carry costs borne by the BBC and ITV. It can shift much of its overhead, either onto parallel production sectors such as commercials, or, as in the case of training, onto the BBC and ITV companies, or indeed onto the social security budget.

5. There are differing accounting practices across the industry and in particular differences in depreciation policies and in the allocation of overheads.

However, the problem of cost comparisons will not go away and what we present here is an outline of the current structure of costs and expenditure drawn from the admittedly inadequate publicly available data. We hope that in the future UK broadcasters will make available fuller cost data. Certainly such data will be necessary if proper public judgement is to be made upon the efficacy of various regulatory and funding arrangements. For instance, such data will be necessary if we are to judge the effect on the industry's cost structure of the 25 percent quotation or the likely effect of a quota for European production as is currently being proposed by the European Commission.

Costs and Quality

A major problem with attempts to impose cost disciplines on the TV production industry in the search for x-efficiency is the difficulty of establishing a clear relationship between cost and quality. In considering this relationship we agree with the view expressed by the accountants, Peat, Marwick, Mitchell in their recent review for the BBC:

> There is an undeniable relationship between quality and money, in the sense that shoddy goods are usually cheap and quality goods are usually expensive. This type of relationship is generally held to exist in broadcasting. In statistical terms the correlation between quality and money is less than one; but its precise value is unmeasurable.
>
> This is an important point, because there is a persistent belief (found not just in many parts of the Corporation, but elsewhere in the artistic world) to the effect that there is a directly proportional relationship between quality and money in broadcasting which necessarily implies that increased money means increased quality and vice versa.
>
> We are conscious that comments on the allocation and management of resources are sometimes perceived as unhelpful because they ignore 'creative considerations' of quality. But we believe that better management of resources can often be achieved without detriment to 'creative considerations' or quality; and indeed can free additional resources which can be deployed directly to programmes. (Peat, Marwick, Mitchell, 1985: Annex p.3)

The problem remains, however, to identify these savings which are not detrimental to quality, and to construct a system which provides incentives both to identify and implement such savings, while at the same time maintaining quality. In an era of increasing cost pressure and international competition in programme supply, all managers, regulators and broadcasting workers will need to take such detailed analysis and its public debate seriously if the quality of broadcasting is not to suffer from cruder methods of cost reduction.

What is clear from a comparison with the United States and a comparison between ITV and BBC is that neither a competitive system nor the introduction of the profit motive solves the problem. Indeed because of the importance of non-price competition and the difficulty of establishing any price relation between quality and the intensity of audience satisfaction (even under Pay TV conditions), competition is likely to raise the general level of costs. And the almost complete absence of competition in the UK between broadcasters for the acquisition of foreign programming has kept such costs, in terms of international comparisons, very low. The recent Italian experience of competition for the acquisition of programmes has increased the cost of bought-in programming by as much as 1000 percent. Moreover, such competition creates much greater unevenness across the schedule, increased expenditure being concentrated on peak-time programming at the expense of programming screened at other times. In general, the savings to be made in direct production costs are difficult to identify and marginal compared with the savings that can be made by altering the scheduling mix and above all by exploiting the economies of scale available on the international market through increased programme purchasing and co-productions.

Programme production is the most substantial component of expenditure on UK television services. The costs of new programmes, whether originated or acquired, are given in Table 2.2.

Table 2.2   *Costs of New Television Programming, 1984 (£ million)*

BBC (network only)[a]	329.9
ITV[b]	375.0
Channel Four	95.4
S4C	24.6
Total	324.9
Total TV expenditure, 1984	1,359.2
New TV programmes as percentage of total TV expenditure	59.1%

[a] The BBC figure is obtained by multiplying the average cost per hour of new network programming (£52,000) by the number of hours of new network programming (6,344).

[b] From the sum of direct and indirect programme expenses are deducted the value of payments made to ITV by Channel Four (£34.8m) and S4C (£17.5m) in order to avoid double accounting.

Sources: BBC Television Facts and Figures 1986; ITCA (1985: 53); *Channel Four Television Company Limited Report and Accounts for the Year Ended 31 March 1986; Sianel Pedwar Cymru Adroddiad Blynyddol A Chyfrifon 1985/86.*

The 63.1 percent of total television expenditure that goes on new television programming contrasts with the figure of 25.5 percent for the typical US TV station (*Broadcasting*, 12 December 1983). Apart from differences due to the use of different ways of accounting for programme costs, this variation is largely to do with the amount of programming that is originated by the television operator, rather than acquired by the operator from another source — it is almost always cheaper to buy a ready-made programme than to make it oneself. UK television operators originate so much of their programming because they are non-profit-maximizing organizations. The BBC is a public service — it is not broadcasting for profit. The ITCA companies are required by the IBA to produce an approved programme mix as a condition of franchise, and Channel Four is owned by the regulator and not run for profit.

The BBC's interpretation of its Royal charter and licence regulation of commercial television by the IBA encourages programme production in three ways:

1. It requires a programme and scheduling mix that operators must produce for themselves. This includes programmes for schools, news, current affairs and local interest programming.

2. It limits the amount of programming acquired from outside the EEC that can be shown.

3. ITV companies are enjoined by the IBA, which grants them their operating franchises, to provide comprehensive production facilities in order to comply with the first requirement and to originate a wide range of programmes besides. The BBC, in compliance with its charter and licence and self-image as a national institution, and in competition with ITV for audiences, originates a comparable amount. UK television services not only transmit originated and acquired television programmes, but also commercials, music promos and feature films.

In the year to 31 March 1986, ITV and Channel Four, according to the IBA annual report, transmitted more than 6300 different commercials. In all 901 hours, or 9.6 percent, of ITV and Channel Four transmissions were taken up by commercials, of which 529 hours were on ITV and 372 hours were on Channel Four. Data are not available for the volume of music promos, some of which are featured in commercials, but it is likely to have exceeded 100 hours across the four channels. In the year to 31 March 1986, feature films from the broadcasters' libraries, for the screening of which broadcasters have acquired rights or which have been funded wholly or in part by the broadcasters, accounted for around 1200 hours of BBC1 and 2432 hours of ITV and 611 hours of Channel Four. Thus material from non-television sources contributed 16.3 percent of UK television transmissions. The costs of producing this material were almost all borne from outside the television industry. The cost of producing these 3200 or so hours is difficult to estimate, not least because the estimated 1500 feature films will have been made over a period of perhaps sixty years, but if we assume their average budget to have been £2 million and that of the commercials and music promos around £50,000, the cost would be in the region of £3.5 billion.

Purchased Programmes

The percentages of transmissions represented by these purchased TV programmes in the year to 31 March 1986 is given in Table 2.3. At 31

Table 2.3   *Percentage of UK TV Transmissions Constituted by UK and Foreign-Acquired TV Programming for the Year to 31 March 1986*

BBC1 and 2 (excluding news and education)[a]	10.2
ITV (excluding TV-am)	12.9
Channel Four	18.9

[a]For the year to 31 March 1985.

Sources: Television, October 1986, p. 235; *IBA Annual Report and Accounts 1985/86*, p. 32; *Channel Four Television Company Limited Report and Accounts for the Year Ended 31 March 1986*, p. 22.

March 1986, according to its annual report, Channel Four's stocks of programmes and film rights stood at £62,684,000, of which £17,169,000 were purchased film rights (including rights for feature films). BBC's stock of purchased programmes was valued in their annual report at £55.3 million.

Repeat Transmissions

UK broadcasters tend to write off the production costs of a programme at the time of first transmission. Repeats are then treated as free. Use of repeats is constrained by three factors. First, the actors' union, Equity, has negotiated terms limiting showings of programmes in which their members appear (all drama) to a window of three years, after which period the broadcasters must obtain the union's consent and pay royalties which increase with the age of the programme. This measure aims (and it succeeds) at discouraging the use of old programmes. Second, the broadcasters have been slow to recognize the value of their old programming, much of which has been destroyed, restricting the catalogue from which they can draw. Third, a consistent finding of audience surveys is that repeats are disliked by viewers.

These constraints are mitigated by several factors, including the 'second life' enjoyed by programming which has not been seen for many years and for which a new audience now exists, the growing differential between the costs of new production and of old programmes notwithstanding the royalties to be paid, and the fashion for nostalgia. These factors have been exploited by Channel Four, especially, with airings of such classics as *Danger Man* and *Ready, Steady, Go* as well as US series like *Bilko* and *The Twilight Zone*.

BBCtv, ITV and Channel Four:
Three Different Sectors

Programme production is only one of a set of functions carried out by UK television broadcasters. These functions are different for each broadcaster (ITV and Channel Four are here referred to as broadcasters, even though, strictly speaking, it is the IBA which broadcasts ITV and Channel Four programmes). To understand programme production costs, it is necessary to put them in the context of the organization's total expenditure. Unfortunately, once put in context, the costs become difficult to compare. It is evident that what each sector counts as programme costs differs in each case.

The BBC

In addition to two networked television channels, the BBC provides regional television programming, local, national and international radio services. The Corporation undertakes news-gathering, monitoring, data transmission, national security duties, audience research, publishing and technical research; it maintains orchestras, archives, libraries and world-wide transmission facilities. It services an array of advisory and representative bodies. It collaborates with the Open University to supply radio and television programmes that are part of the OU's courses. Total expenditure in the year to 31 March 1986 was £908.1 million.

In its 1986 annual report, the BBC attributed £582.1 million of its expenditure to television. It painstakingly attributes central and shared costs to each of its services. This process of attribution is nevertheless arbitrary. For example, if the BBC decides to improve one of its regional production centres, the director of finance will discuss with the managing directors for television and radio how much each will contribute from their budgets towards the cost of the work. Radio and television then negotiate the amount and the timetable for payment. If radio stands to gain more from the work, or it has surplus money available, it may choose to pay more than its 'share' in order to ensure that the desired facilities are available by a desired date. Radio regards this as sufficiently important to cover some of television's costs, in the knowledge that in another instance the situation might be reversed and television will cover some of radio's costs. Such arrangements will distort BBC cost attribution between the services.

The ITV Companies

Although the ITV companies suggested in their Peacock submission

(ITCA, 1985: 9) that 'the ITV system was not designed primarily with considerations of cost-effectiveness in mind', the companies themselves are in the business of profit-maximization. They make money by selling advertising time and programmes, and programme costs are part of the costs of the sale of advertising time, their principal source of revenue.

But if they wish to have their IBA franchises renewed, they must forego some of their profit in order to comply with regulations on quantity, quality and content of output. There is some room for manoeuvre: the IBA, both in judging between franchise applicants and in enforcing the terms of the franchises, has to be able to make judgements on the effects on the financial health of an ITV company of imposing a given set of programming requirements. Nevertheless, the ITV companies are encouraged by the franchise terms and by the way they are taxed to be seen to spend on programming. They will tend to make more expensive programmes than either the BBC or Channel Four; they must bring every resource available to bear on maximizing audience appeal in order to achieve high ratings and attract more, and more expensive, advertising; they will also attribute costs and carry out accounting in order to make their programming *appear* as expensive as possible. In this way they are satisfying the advertisers and the IBA, which has never in its history criticized an ITV company for excessive expenditure (though mandated to monitor expenditure), and they are also minimizing levy payments.

The ITV companies have also been encouraged, by the IBA and by the government, to sell their programmes overseas. This imposes an obligation to make programmes that will have an international appeal, especially in North America and hence tends to raise production values and costs.

Channel Four

Channel Four operates on a different basis from the BBC and the ITV companies. It exists to commission and buy programming with which it programmes the channel.

Channel Four does engage in other activities, such as computer software design and marketing and the selling of programmes overseas. More significantly it has become one of the UK's leading film producers through its subsidiary, Film on Four International (FFI). The rationale of FFI is that it enables feature films to be made of the type and character that Channel Four, in accordance with its brief to show innovative programming, would like to show.

Channel Four maintains only the most limited production facilities and its staff is involved only in organizing and marketing its television channel. Its overheads and capital assets are correspondingly small.

When Channel Four commissions work from an independent producer, it pays the producer's overheads only over the life of the project. It encourages producers to negotiate super-competitive rates with facilities and post-production houses, often at marginal and even below-marginal costs, since all parties know that Channel Four budgets will not allow for payment of the sort of rates paid by the producer of a television commercial or an industrial training film. Channel Four also exploits the surplus of companies seeking commissions over the number of commissions made, to strengthen its negotiating position. Like Marks and Spencer in the retailing sector, Channel Four, in order to promote programme diversity, will periodically end a longstanding relationship with a producer. This has the added effect of instilling cost discipline and discouraging complacency.

Also pushing down Channel Four programme prices, and consequently the sector's production costs, is the substantial use of purchased material. Channel Four is seldom in the same market for programmes as BBC and ITV, or indeed broadcasters in other countries, and obtains programming at very favourable rates. The ITV companies and the independent producers know that Channel Four will not be starved of product if it is challenged to raise its budgets for originated material.

The differences between the structures of each sector, the costs of producing programmes and the different incentives to limit expenditure, make comparisons between the sectors difficult, if not impossible. This difficulty is compounded by the vastly divergent ways in which each sector does its accounts — the BBC nowhere describes how much it spends on programme production, only how much goes on staff wages and other such items from which programme costs cannot be extracted; the ITV companies split their expenditure between direct and indirect programme costs and operate an artificial pricing system for exchanging programmes between one another; the situation is such that the IBA has given up trying to establish an average cost per hour for ITV output. Only Channel Four states how much it paid for what sort of programming, but the price paid may or may not correspond to its cost.

BBC Television Costs

The period covered in this survey of BBC television costs and output is from 1 April 1978 to 31 March 1985, chosen because much of the data are only available for those years. The sources, unless otherwise stated, are *BBC Annual Reports and Handbooks*, and *BBC Television Facts and Figures*.

As has been suggested above, attribution of costs by the BBC to television generally, and to television production specifically, is subject to the accounting policies employed. In its most recent accounts (*BBC Annual Report and Handbook 1987*), figures for 1984/85 were restated. A comparison of the two sets of accounts is given in Table 2.4.

Table 2.4   *A Comparison of BBC Expenditure Figures for the Year to 31 March 1985 (£ million, except staff numbers)*

Item	1985 Audit Report	1986 Audit Report
Total BBC income	731.8	732.1
Total operating expenditure	675.3	738.5
Total capital expenditure	99.5	60.1
Depreciation	n.a.	(25.5)
Total expenditure	774.8	773.1
Deficit of income over expenditure	−43.0	−41.0
TV operating expenditure	493.0	533.9
TV capital expenditure	61.6	n.a.
Total TV expenditure	554.6	533.9
Radio operating expenditure	182.3	203.5
Radio capital expenditure	37.9	n.a.
Total radio expenditure	220.2	203.5
Interest payable (−)	−0.3	−1.1
Number of TV staff	17,992	17.992
TV production and other staff costs	286.6	296.3
Other expenses	18.8	20.7
Depreciation	—	18.3
Minor acquisitions	—	11.0
All other TV operating expenditure	187.6	187.6

This comparison gives an indication of the impact of accounting practices; in the first set of figures, for every £1 spent on radio, £2.52 was spent on television; while in the second set, for every £1 spent on radio, £2.62 was spent on television. Costs have been shifted from capital to operating expenditure, and staff costs for radio and television have increased by 3.9 percent, from £388 million to £403.3 million, even though the number of employees (25,163) has remained the same. Inadequate explanation is given for these restatements — that is, where any explanation is given at all. For purposes of comparison with earlier years, the figures originally given for the year 1984/85 are used here.

Table 2.5   *Total BBCtv Expenditure as a Percentage of Total BBC Home Services Expenditure, 1978/79 to 1984/85*

Year to 31 Mar	Total BBC Expenditure (£ million)	Total TV Expenditure (£ million)	Total TV Expenditure as % of Total BBC Expenditure (%)
1979	324.4	231.8	71.5
1980	409.4	293.5	71.7
1981	465.7	331.4	71.2
1982	538.3	382.1	71.0
1983	634.8	458.5	72.2
1984	721.1	520.4	72.2
1985	774.8	554.6	71.6

Table 2.5 sets out expenditure on television in relation to total BBC expenditure. From these figures it is evident that television takes a stable proportion of total BBC expenditure. In Table 2.6 expenditure on new network programmes (originated and acquired) is shown. This presents a different picture. The BBC has only ever published figures on new network programme expenditure. It is not possible therefore to examine how costs for regional programming have behaved. Moreover, the figures given here (taken from *BBC Television Facts and Figures*) are far from dependable. Nevertheless, the picture emerges of considerable fluctuation in programme expenditure.

Table 2.6   *Expenditure on New Network Programming (excluding Open University) as a Percentage of Total BBCtv Expenditure*

Year to 31 Mar	New Network Programmes (hrs)	Average Cost per Hour (£)	Total Cost New Network Programmes (£m)	Total Cost as % of Total BBCtv Spend (%)
1979	5224	24,000	125.4	54.1
1980	5484	31,000	170.0	57.9
1981	5386	34,000	183.1	55.2
1982	5879	41,000	241.0	63.1
1983	5818	47,000	273.4	59.6
1984	6205	47,000	291.6	56.0
1985	6389	52,000	332.2	59.9

The major item in BBC television accounts is production and other staff costs. In considering these it is worth keeping in mind the number of staff attributed to television. These data, along with the average cost per member of staff, are given in Table 2.7. Do shifts in staff costs help to explain the shifts in programme production expenditure? Table 2.8 compares changes in new network programme expenditure to changes in total TV staff costs and in average costs per member of staff. It is apparent from these calculations that staff costs, though they are the largest item of expenditure and are a significant factor in production costs, do not explain either the magnitude or the pattern of increase in new network production costs.

Income and Overall Expenditure 1978/79 to 1984/85
Between 1978/79 and 1984/85, the TV licence fee rose in steps, from £21 to £46 for a colour licence, and from £9 to £15 for a monochrome

Table 2.7   *BBC Television Staff Costs, Staff Numbers and Average Costs per Member of Staff*

Year to 31 Mar	TV Production and Other Staff Costs (£m)	Number of TV Staff[a]	Average Cost per Member of Staff (£)
1979	118.6	16,214	7,315
1980	151.7	17,027	8,909
1981	179.7	16,796	10,700
1982	203.8	17,009	11,982
1983	230.1	17,589	13,082
1984	259.7	17,679	14,690
1985	286.6	17,992	15,929

[a]Staff numbers for 1978/79 to 1981/82 are estimates.

Table 2.8   *Comparison in Changes of New Network Programming Costs, TV Staff Costs, and Average Costs Per Member of Staff (percent)*

Year to 31 Mar	Change in New Network Programme Expenditure	Change in TV Staff Costs	Change in Average Cost per Staff Member
1980	+ 35.6	+ 27.9	+ 21.8
1981	+ 7.7	+ 18.5	+ 20.1
1982	+ 31.6	+ 13.4	+ 12.0
1983	+ 13.4	+ 12.9	+ 9.2
1984	+ 6.7	+ 12.9	+ 12.3
1985	+ 13.9	+ 10.4	+ 8.4
Total increase over period	+164.9	+141.7	+117.8

licence. The income to the BBC from the licence fee, however, has risen at a steady rate because of a progressive shift from monochrome to colour licences. The average annual rate of increase over the seven years was 15.13 percent. Total income after tax rose from £315.5 million to £731.8 million at an average annual rate of increase of 15.45 percent. Television expenditure, including capital expenditure (the largest proportion of which goes on replacing equipment) rose from £231.8 million to £554.6 million at an average annual rate of increase of 15.82 percent.

Included in television expenditure are directorate costs allocated to television or radio on a fairly arbitrary basis: in 1985/86 a figure of £3,660 per member of staff was used for most of radio while the figure for TV was £1,500 per member of staff. Whereas TV operating expenditure for 1983/84 was given in the BBC annual report as £450.3 million, Peat, Marwick cited a figure of £277.6 million which excluded the costs of engineering, central support, network production centres (NPCs) and regions. It is presumably also an accounting decision that determines how costs in these three areas are allocated to TV. The Peat, Marwick figure is less than the £291.6 million spent on new network production shown by BBCtv in that year (see Table 2.6 above) because it excludes the costs of the regionally-based NPCs.

Expenditure on New Network Programming
The number of hours of new network programming, excluding Open University, continuity and trailers, rose from 5044 to 6344, at an average annual rate of increase of 3.93 percent. The average cost per hour of new network programming rose from £24,000 to £52,000 at an average annual rate of increase of 14.12 percent. These two elements combined to increase expenditure on new network programming from £125.4 million to £332.2 million. The average annual rate of increase was 18.15 percent.

The Volume of Transmissions
We have already seen that the volume of new network productions transmitted by the BBC has risen at an average annual rate of 3.93 percent over the seven years. In the same period the total volume of transmissions (including the BBC's contribution of S4C and Open University programmes) has risen from 12,168 hours to 14,398 hours, an average annual rate of increase of 2.88 percent. Much of the increase occurred in the last two years, 1983/84 and 1984/85, with the introduction of breakfast television. In the year 1986/87 an increase of around 1.8 percent will be attributable to the introduction of daytime

television (in the following year the increase will be of the order of 7.1 percent).

Cost increases arising from growth in the volume of transmissions may be offset by increasing the volume of repeat transmissions, purchased material and lower-cost programming. Such scheduling will reduce the marginal cost of programming. This was indeed the case in 1983/84 when the average cost per hour of new network production was held at £47,000, the 1982/83 level, a reduction in real terms (allowing for inflation) of 4.49 percent. However, in the following year, the average cost per hour rose to £52,000. Average costs per hour of new network production are likely to be £56,300 in 1985/86 and £57,700 in 1986/87, an average annual rate of increase of 5.38 percent.

The Cost of Acquired Programming

The average annual rate of increase of acquired programming is the highest for any new programme category. The average cost per hour rose from £7,000 to £26,000 over the seven years, an average annual rate of increase of 24.75 percent. The average cost per hour of acquired programming is now greater than that of sport and possibly of current affairs. The BBC reduced the amount of new acquired material from 624 hours in the year 1978/79 to 546 hours in 1984/85.

Labour Costs within the BBC

While the BBC's annual accounts itemize production and other staff costs for television, in the same year numbers of staff employed are not broken down between television and radio. For those years estimations for numbers of TV staff have been made. Payments to freelance and temporary staff are not itemized separately, but total wage costs, including freelance and temporary staff have been divided by numbers of TV staff to produce a figure for average labour costs per member of staff.

Peat, Marwick gave total TV staff in 1983/84 as 9265. The figure in the annual report was 17,679. For 1985/86, BBC Schedules for the Allocation of Costs (including Accommodation) gave a total TV staff size of 6616. For the purpose of this study, the annual report figures for the seven years are used, as stated or else estimated on the basis of total BBC staff numbers.

Between 1978/79 and 1984/85 the number of TV staff rose from 16,214 to 17,992, an average annual rate of increase of 1.77 percent. Average costs per member of staff rose from £7315 to £15,929, an average annual rate of increase of 13.96 percent. Taking increase in staff numbers and increase in average costs per staff member, we obtain an average annual rate of increase in labour costs of 15.97 percent. Though this rate of increase is marginally greater than that for TV expenditure as a whole (15.82 percent), it is significantly less than the rate of increase for new network programming costs (18.15 percent).

In Table 2.9 the average annual rate of increase for each BBC programme category is given. All but three of the programme

Table 2.9   *Average Cost per Hour by Network TV Programme Category, 1978/79 to 1984/85*

Programme Category	Range (£)	Annual Rate of Increase (%)
Acquired programming	7–26,000	24.75
Drama	89–278,000	20.99
Features, music and documentaries	29–78,000	19.45
Educational	29–75,000	17.51
Religious	20–48,000	16.09
Sport	11–25,000	15.44
Light entertainment	45–95,000	13.80
Children's	22–45,000	13.34
Current affairs	18–26,000	6.98
Average cost per hour	24–52,000	14.12
Total expenditure on new programming	125.4–332.2m	18.15

Omitted from this table are the following categories: outside broadcast events, news and Asian/community. Average costs per hour of outside broadcast events and Asian/community are only given from 1980/81 on; for news from 1983/84 on.

categories' average costs per hour have risen more than the average cost per hour for new network productions as a whole. The three which have risen less have benefited from savings achieved through video technology and increased studio use. Current affairs has also benefited from what can only be described as economies of scale: between 1978/79 and 1983/84 hours of network current affairs programming grew from 605 to 1485, dropping back to 1396 in 1984/85. The average annual rate of increase in hours over the full seven years was 15.88 percent (compared to 3.98 percent for new network production as a whole).

Economies of scale might also be held to operate in the case of sports programming. Sports have represented a consistently high proportion of all new network output. Sports programming costs are also reduced by changes in sports covered. Snooker, darts and bowls are sports that have received increasing coverage in recent years. The quality of coverage of snooker, darts and bowls does not suffer from more limited shooting and editing facilities than ice skating, basketball or gymnastics, say, might entail; for them the area to be covered is greater and the action moves more. Another economy made with the new sports coverage is the long duration of events covered: if crew and presenters can stay put for as much as two weeks (in the case of the World Professional Snooker Championship), spending a great deal of that time shooting finished programming, the savings in downtime and travel, not to mention in alternative and undoubtedly more expensive programming, are likely to be high.

To recap, between 1978/79 and 1984/85, BBC television expenditure rose at an average annual rate of 15.82 percent. General inflation, as represented by the RPI, rose at an average annual rate of 10.24 percent. The difference between these two figures — 5.58 percent — might be defined as BBCtv broadcasting inflation.

So far as this analysis of BBC figures goes, the case that the major contributory factor in broadcasting inflation is labour costs does not appear to be true. Whether this is true for the industry as a whole would require more extensive data than are presently available. The BBC labour costs include freelance and permanent staff but not performers. On the data available it seems that the average annual rate of increase in labour costs per member of staff was 13.96 percent according to figures in the BBC annual reports, 13.20 percent according to the sample of TV production costs examined as part of this study. The average annual rate of increase in the number of TV staff was 1.77 percent, considerably less than the rate of increase of either total hours of TV transmissions (2.88 percent) or of new network productions (3.93 percent). It is clear that non-labour costs have risen at least as quickly as labour costs.

The figure for broadcasting inflation of 5.58 percent might best be interpreted as being a function of the following factors:
— increases in the volume of transmissions and of new network production
— increases in the cost of acquired programming
— increases in the cost of film and video stock, equipment and processing that are outstripping general inflation
— increases in the scope of administrative and managerial tasks corresponding to growth in BBCtv activities
— increases in programme production values and the attendant increases in the demand for labour and for externally-supplied goods and services

Data published by the BBC are not adequate to permit quantification of these increases. This would be desirable since, by weighting the increase factors, the BBC would be able to mount stronger arguments for improved funding. The BBC could also, on the basis of such analysis, improve allocative efficiency by taking decisions on resources and expenditure aimed towards their optimization.

ITV

The ITV sector is more opaque than the BBC. No data on programme costs are published beyond those for total programme expenditure for all the ITV companies. Rough details of what the ITV companies regard as their programme expenditure are given in the *ITV Handbook*, published by the IBA. In addition, the IBA annual reports provide a breakdown of the origin of transmissions. In submissions to the Peacock inquiry, additional financial data were provided.

ITV companies do prepare detailed budgets, providing useful insights into the allocation of resources, but these are considered highly confidential. For this examination of ITV production costs, we have drawn on one such budget for one of the network companies covering the year to 31 March 1985, supplemented by the data on Thames Television published in Manuel Alvarado and John Stewart's book, *Made for Television: Euston Films Limited* (1985)

The ITV companies obtain around 95 percent of their revenue from the sale of about 10 percent of their and Channel Four's airtime to advertisers. Agency fees and commissions are deducted and the companies are left with the balance, the so-called net advertising revenue (NAR). Each of the companies is responsible for selling airtime in its region. The exceptions are Channel TV whose sales are handled by the ITV contractor for the south-west, TSW, and LWT and Thames who share between them the London region, Thames selling weekday airtime (until 5.45 pm on Fridays) and LWT selling Friday evenings and weekends. TV-am is the only national advertiser, since Channel Four airtime is sold by each region separately.

Because some regions are much larger or richer than others, so are some of the companies. Five of the richest companies — Central, Granada, LWT, Thames and Yorkshire — who between them accounted in 1984 for 60 percent of NAR, produced, in the year to 31 March 1986, 45.5 percent of ITV networked and part-networked programming, that is, nearly five times as much as the ten 'regional' companies. The regional companies are split into two tiers, 'large regionals' — Anglia, HTV, Scottish TV, TVS and Tyne Tees (with 33 percent of NAR in 1984) — and 'small regionals' — Border TV, Channel TV, Grampian TV, TSW and Ulster TV (with 6.5 percent of NAR in 1984). One of the 'large regionals', TVS, is actually richer than Yorkshire TV, the smallest of the network companies.

The fifteen ITV companies, joined by TV-am which, since 1983, has had the franchise for breakfast television on ITV, form the Independent Television Companies Association (ITCA). Though most originated programming is produced by one or other region, some, the so-called 'network events', are produced with monies paid into a pool by the network companies. In 1984/85 there were forty-one hours of such programming, mainly sports, party and TUC conferences and election coverage, produced or acquired at a cost of £5,280,000, an average cost per hour of £129,000. In sports there have been undoubted rises in the costs of production. The fees for the coverage of athletics rose from £250,000 per year in 1980 to £2.1 million per annum (£10.5 million for five years) in 1985 (*The Observer Magazine* 1 March 1987, pp. 27–8). It is clear that the cost of all the factors of production are not under the control of the TV companies.

Independent Television News (ITN), which is owned by the ITV companies, in the year to 31 March 1985 cost around £38 million and produced around 572 hours of programming, at an average cost of £60,400 per hour. *Channel Four News* was priced at £33,500 per hour and ITV's network news at £87,600 per hour.

This price variation results from a complex system of transfer pricing for the exchange of programmes within ITV which is designed to subsidize the smaller regional companies and even out revenue and programme expenditure across the network. Simon Domberger and Julian Middleton (1985: 30) describe the ITV structure thus:

> Each company pays entirely for the programmes it makes for transmission, but the 'Big Five' [the network companies] share in the cost of programmes that are networked. This has the effect of subsidising the smaller companies [the regionals] — those with fewer viewers and hence lower advertising revenues. The amount each company pays for network productions is calculated on the basis of its share of the Net Advertising Revenue After Levy (NARAL) earned by the entire ITV system.

The ITV Programme Tariff System

The scope of the cross-subsidy effect mentioned by Domberger and Middleton can be seen in the figures for ITV income and expenditure for the year ended 31 December 1984, prepared by the IBA and published in ITCA's submission to the Peacock inquiry (ITCA, 1985: 53).

From these accounts we see that ITV companies bore direct and indirect programme costs on their own productions of £427 million. Of these, £296.7 million (69.5 percent) were borne by the network companies, £108 million (25.3 percent) by the large regionals, and £22.3 million (5.2 percent) by the small regionals, while the proportions of NAR were 60 percent for the network companies, 33 percent for the large regionals and 6.5 percent for the small regionals.

There then ensues a procedure for exchanging programmes between the companies. The ITV companies determine the total value of the seven-day pool to cover Category A programme exchange. Category A consists of those ITV-originated programmes shown simultaneously by all the regions. In the year to 31 March 1985 the pool was given a value estimated as £172.5 million. Into this pool the regionals were to pay £49.5 million. (In the figures published by ITCA, the regionals' contribution in 1984 was £49.2 million.)

The companies then exchange programmes between one another based on tariff values given to each programme and series. The result of this exchange in 1984 was that the networks paid out £21.8 million, and received £55.3 million; the large regionals paid out £46.5 million and received £27 million; and the small regionals paid out £8.6 million and received £1.2 million. The tariff rates at which programmes were exchanged in 1984/85 are given in Table 2.10. To provide one point of comparison, the average cost per hour cited by the BBC in that year is also given.

The greatest disparity between ITV tariff value and BBC programme cost exists for the following categories: children's; current affairs,

Table 2.10   *ITV Category A Programme Tariffs, 1984/85*

Programme Category	Tariff per Hour (£)	BBC Cost per Hour (£)
Adult education	68,000	75,000
Children's	72–180,000	45,000
Current affairs, features and documentaries	120–134,000	26–78,000
Drama	255,000	278,000
Light entertainment	100–255,000	95,000
Religion	90,000	48,000
Schools	103,000	75,000
Sports and outside broadcasts	60–190,000	25–45,000

features and documentaries; light entertainment; religion; and sports and outside broadcasts. Children's, current affairs, features and documentaries, and religion are categories of programming on which the IBA lays great stress, making sure that, in both amount and quality, they conform to the standards of public service broadcasting. The schools category, which the IBA regards similarly, does not emerge as an area of disparity because its programmes are often repeats, so that the ITV company supplying the programmes will receive credit each time they are aired; the ITV/BBC disparity may in fact be greater here than for any programme category. Light entertainment and sports are categories on which the ITV system itself lays great stress, since they are essential components in a successful, audience-pulling schedule.

ITV Labour Costs

Because ITV companies distinguish between direct and indirect programme costs, and only direct costs are attributed to specific programmes, it is impossible to determine how much a given programme costs. The exceptions to this rule are programmes produced by ITV subsidiaries that are effectively bought-in by the network. *Minder* and *Widows*, produced by Euston Films, and the animated children's programmes made by Cosgrave Hall (both companies are subsidiaries of Thames Television) are good examples. In 1983/84 Euston's expenditure on 29.5 hours of filmed drama, excluding administrative costs of £355,000, was £7,785,000, giving an average cost per 52-minute episode of £264,000. In the following year the average cost per episode (excluding overheads) had dropped to around £236,000. The tariff rate at which this programming was exchanged was £255,000.

It is impossible to say how much of Euston's programme costs were overheads. But given the structure of Euston as described by Alvarado and Stewart (1985), its overhead costs are likely to be considerably lower than those of an ITV company. At the ITV company examined, however, there were in 1984/85 2287 employees of whom 1624 were classified as production staff. Production staff salaries, wages and other expenses were £30,944,978, in addition to which there were company pension contributions and a staff bonus, estimated at £6,519,000, and personnel costs estimated at £990,000. Freelance production personnel cost £1,562,265. This means that production staff costs were £40,016,243. Average annual cost per full-time member of the production staff (excluding freelance) was £23,680. Average annual payroll costs for production staff, that is, salaries and overtime, were £18,551. The figure for the company as a whole was £17,950. This is 12.7 percent higher than 1984/85 average *total* staff costs per member of staff at the BBC, of £15,929.

Programme Costs

In the year 1984/85, the ITV company examined transmitted 707 hours of new programming which it had produced itself. The total *direct* cost was £26,017,000 and the average cost per hour was £37,000. Indirect programme costs added £38,067,000 and the average cost per hour, accordingly, was £90,600.

Production output by this company can be broken down and compared with BBCtv's for the same period. This breakdown is given in Table 2.11. Some of the programme categories will be constituted differently in each case, so this comparison is intended only as a rough guide. The ITV company's mix of programmes is quite different from the BBC's, with high-price categories, like drama and light entertainment, being better represented in the ITV company's schedule than in BBC's.

This comparison with the BBC can be made for the whole ITV network schedule. Figures are shown in Table 2.12. Again, it must be kept in mind that the programme categories are differently constituted in each case. And again, the differences in programme mix are striking. Against this background, comparisons of overall expenditure on programmes may not be as revealing as it is often thought.

The ITV system has developed to meet certain financial and regulatory demands which are not present in the UK TV system as a whole. These demands — to meet franchise conditions imposed by the

Table 2.11   *Comparison of an ITV Company's and the BBC's Output of New Own-Produced Programming, 1984/85*

Programme Category	ITV Company (% of Total)	BBC Network TV (% of Total)
All new own-produced programming	100.0	100.0
Adult education	5.8	n.a.
Children's	12.3	7.8
Current affairs, features and documentaries	17.1	38.4
Adult drama	8.1	5.5
Light entertainment	17.8	7.8
Religion	1.5	1.8
Schools	2.5	5.9
Sports and outside broadcasts	11.6	27.0

Sources: the ITV company's budget, 1984/85; *BBC Television Facts and Figures 1986*.

Table 2.12 *Comparison of ITV Transmissions (excluding TV-am) and BBC Network Output, 1985/86*

Programme Category	ITV (% of Total)	BBC Network TV (% of Total)
All programming	100.0	100.0
Adult education	1.6	3.5
Children's	11.3	7.3
Current affairs, news and news magazines, features and documentaries	18.8	27.6
Adult drama, acquired films and film series	30.0	20.3
Light entertainment and music	12.5	8.3
Religion	2.3	1.6
Schools	6.5	4.8
Sports	7.7[a]	14.4
Continuity		3.6
Advertising	9.5	—
Open University	—	8.6

[a] Includes sports and continuity.

Sources: IBA Annual Report 1986; BBC Annual Report and Handbook 1987.

IBA and to minimize tax liabilities on behalf of the companies' shareholders — have led to curious accounting practices which disguise how costs and resources are allocated. In this light, sweeping statements about relative costs seem unwise.

Channel Four

With the establishment of Channel Four many substantial and far-reaching changes in UK broadcasting ecology occurred. These extended from the creation of an outlet for independently-financed and produced television programmes — which revolutionized the opportunities of such independent production — to the creation of a television market in the UK for non-English language programmes acquired from overseas.

The Channel Four company was set up by the Independent Broadcasting Authority under Section 12(2) of the Broadcasting Act 1981 to 'obtain and assemble the necessary material and to carry out such other activities involved in providing programmes for the fourth channel television service as appears to the IBA to be appropriate'. It derives its income from the IBA, on the basis of subscriptions received by the IBA from the ITV companies. In return, it is the ITV companies that sell advertising on Channel Four (and derive income from it). The companies also receive payments from Channel Four for programming supplied, some of which is original programming and some of which is programming already shown on ITV. In the year ending 31 March 1986, the ITV companies paid to the IBA subscriptions of £174,498,000, of which £129.1 million was paid to Channel Four. They obtained £112.6 million in advertising revenues from it (up by 50 percent, from £75.2 million, compared with the previous year), as well as £36.1 million from programme sales. Hence the net benefit of Channel Four to the ITV system was £19.6 million.

Another element of the equation to be weighed up is that producing for Channel Four entailed the additional use of existing production capacity, thereby reducing production costs of programmes for transmission on ITV. A case in point is ITN which, while earning an additional £7.2 million in 1983/84, over and above its turnover for its ITV operation, from the sale of *Channel Four News*, only increased its total operating expenditure by £5.5 million.

The essential difference between Channel Four and either the BBC or ITV is that it is a channel operator with virtually no in-house production staff. In practice, the precedent for this existed with the non-network or regional ITV companies (which acquire the bulk of their programming from the five network companies or through the centralized ITV programme acquisition body run by Leslie Halliwell). The distinction was that Channel Four was to commission the major part of its programming from ITV contractors and from independent producers.

Two separate questions are to be dealt with here. The first is the extent to which the creation of Channel Four has improved the economies of programme production for the ITV companies and, allied to this, the extent to which the advent of Channel Four has created an increased demand on the productive capacities of the companies. The second question relates to the ways in which the extent and nature of the growth of the independent sector has been determined by the needs of Channel Four, and as those needs have changed, the manner in which the independent sector has changed.

The analysis of the data compiled on Channel Four is insufficient to describe production there in the same terms and with the same precision as was possible with the BBC and ITV. Given its decentralized structure, Channel Four programme production is extremely hard to account for.

What we do know, from the Channel Four report and accounts and from a breakdown of 1984/85 output provided by Channel Four (the two do not altogether coincide), is that the ITCA companies, including ITN, supplied 1065 slot-hours of new programming to Channel Four in the period (slot-hours, unlike running time, include commercials, trailers and continuity). ITN's *Channel Four News* (239 slot-hours) and 'other entertainment' (242 slot-hours) accounted for 45 percent. New, independently-produced programming provided 690 slot-hours, of which drama and the arts (144 slot-hours), sports (102 hours), current affairs (116 hours) and 'other entertainment' (101 hours) made up 67 percent.

The cost ('transmission expenditure') of the independent programming was £38.7 million. The cost of the ITCA companies' programming was £31.7 million. In addition Channel Four paid £2.9 million to the ITCA companies, and £0.3 million to independent production companies, for rebroadcast rights to 332 hours of programming, of which 221 hours, or two-thirds, were drama and arts or 'other entertainment'. The complete breakdown, supplied by Channel Four, is given in Table 2.13.

In the year to 31 March 1986, total transmission expenditure had increased by £5.9 million (6.2 percent) to £101.3 million, of which £39.4 million (up by 1 percent) was paid to independents and £36.1 million (up by 4.3 percent) to ITCA companies. Acquired material and feature films accounted for £17.3 million (up by 7.5 percent) and programme-related costs for £8.5 million (up by 49.1 percent). Channel Four produced one programme, *Right to Reply*, whose costs are not itemized but presumably are included in 'programme-related costs'.

According to the *Channel Four Report and Accounts 1985*, 313 companies contributed to the 690 hours of programming. (This is only a notional figure, given that the report actually says that Channel Four 'made programme payments to 313 Independent Production Companies (1984, 281 companies)'; this does not mean that the payments related to programmes transmitted in 1984/85.) However, a small number of companies was responsible for a large proportion of those hours: Action Time (with a turnover of £375,341 and with four employees) produced 24 hours; Brook Productions produced 38 hours (mainly of current affairs); Chatsworth produced 18 hours of 'other entertainment'; Cheerleader supplied 84 hours of sports; Diverse provided 19 hours; and Goldcrest, in association with Antenne 2, supplied 13 hours of *The Living Body*, and, in association with WGBH (a Boston public broadcasting service (PBS) station) and Comworld, 4 hours of *Concealed Enemies*. Griffin contributed 14 hours, and Holmes Associates 19 hours of 'other entertainment'. Limehouse Productions, the largest independent production company (with the largest

Table 2.13　*Channel Four Analysis of Transmission Expenditure by Category for the Year to 31 March 1985*

	Commissioned				Bought In (purchased and pre-purchased)		Repeats		Total	
	ITCA		Independent							
	(hours)	(£m)	(hours)	(£m)	(hours)	(£m)	(hours)	(£m)	(hours)	(£m)
Drama and arts	46	2.6	144	13.5	270	4.2	171	2.1	631	22.4
Other entertainment	242	8.0	101	7.0	198	1.9	50	0.6	591	17.5
Sport	116	1.4	102	3.2	29	0.4	6	—	253	5.0
News	239	8.0	—	—	—	—	—	—	239	8.0
Current affairs	163	1.7	116	4.1	—	—	3	—	282	5.8
Education	137	4.9	109	4.2	60	1.4	72	0.3	378	10.8
Religion	43	1.5	10	0.2	8	0.1	3	0.1	64	1.9
Documentaries	33	1.2	40	2.8	106	1.7	25	0.1	204	5.8
11th hour and multi-cultural	38	1.9	61	3.5	60	0.6	2	—	161	6.0
Feature films and cartoons	8	0.5	7	0.2	775	5.8	—	—	790	6.5
Total	1065	31.7	690	38.7	1506[a]	16.1	332	3.2	3593	89.7

[a] Includes 114 hours of repeats.

Source: Channel Four Report and Accounts 1985.

operating losses), produced 14 hours of *The Business Programme*, 9 hours of *The Old Country* and 4 hours of studio drama, not to mention 2 hours of documentaries and a half-hour segment of *Dance on Four*, to make a total of 29.5 hours. Siddharta Productions, with its series for the elderly, *Years Ahead*, produced 22 hours; while Telekation, with children's and features programming, produced 18 hours. Sports Sponsorship International and TransWorld International between them contributed the 17 hours of sports that Cheerleader did not produce. And one company, Mersey Television, the producers of *Brookside*, made 52 hours. Mersey has a highly unusual relationship with Channel Four which, according to Mersey's accounts, reimburses production costs in full. In 1985 Mersey, based in Liverpool, employed eighty-six staff, of whom sixty-five were technicians and production crew.

The fourteen companies listed above accounted for 371 hours, or 54 percent, of the 690 hours of new programming. Two other major contractors, Humphrey Barclay Associates and Petrofilms, were responsible for drama series — *Relative Strangers* and *The Irish R.M.* respectively.

The picture that therefore emerges is of nearly 300 companies contributing a little over an hour of programming each. For this statistic to make any sense, a considerable number of these companies will be partners in co-productions. However, the fact remains that, even if half were production partners, and the average amount of programming two hours, rather than one hour, over the year, this is an insufficient volume of work to sustain even the smallest outfit beyond the lifetime of one particular production.

In 1985 Channel Four dramatically rationalized its command and control systems. It took away programme contracts from some long-term suppliers (like Large Door), and put others (Brook and Diverse) on a more provisional footing. This process has been described by an independent producer as one whereby Channel Four's commissioning editors (responsible for various categories of programming) become executive producers and the Channel Four cost-controllers (whose numbers have swelled and powers increased) become the effective producers. In this structure the independent producers become effectively employees of the channel, except that they enjoy no long-term security or benefits.

The average cost per hour of Channel Four's independently-produced programming in 1985/86 was approximately £40,500, down from £45,500 in the previous year. The average cost per hour of new and repeated programming supplied by the ITV companies and ITN to

Channel Four in 1985/86 was £33,400, up from 28,000 in the previous year.

The massive variation between the cost to Channel Four of ITV programming, and the cost to ITV of its own programming (see p. 40) is attributable to the special relationship between the channel and ITV. When Channel Four invites tenders for commissions from the ITV companies, it is able to encourage the lowest possible bids since the ITV companies know that any number of independent companies would offer to produce the programme. This encourages the ITV companies to quote prices effectively based on the marginal cost of producing the programme. There are three reasons why they do this: first, they will be using spare capacity that might otherwise go unused, so the marginal cost is indeed the correct price for them to charge; second, they are unwilling to forgo production offers from Channel Four since this would stimulate still further the independents; and third, it is irrelevant how much they charge Channel Four since Channel Four will be paying the ITV companies with money received from the ITV companies. If therefore, the ITV companies were to be allowed to charge more for the programming they supply, it would give rise to the demand from Channel Four, via the IBA, for the ITV subscriptions to Channel Four to be increased.

The programmes supplied by ITV to Channel Four will, on the whole, be less costly to produce than those shown on ITV, so strict comparison between programme prices is not in order. The bulk of the programming will fall into the less expensive categories, like news, sport, current affairs and 'other entertainment' — in this case quiz programmes like *Countdown*.

The low cost of the independently-produced programming stems from the very low overheads incurred by the producers (and passed on to Channel Four), the use of facilities houses at a heavily discounted rate (all facilities houses indulge in loss-leading, on the basis of their ability to recoup with commercials, industrial videos and music promos) and the fact that, unlike the BBC and the ITV companies, there is no allocation of resources to the long-term maintenance of the company.

Even among the larger suppliers surveyed, one, Court House Films, was mortgaged to Channel Four; another, Bright Thoughts, was mortgaged to the bank and another, Imago Films, made a loss, and yet another, Picture Partnership, was in liquidation. Fourteen others considered themselves too small to have filed any accounts since their incorporation.

Very few measures of productivity can distinguish between

programmes made cheaply and cheap programmes. The Channel Four system relies on both. In many ways it is in more of a monopoly position than the other broadcasters since it alone provides funding for so much of independent production. As described above, Channel Four from its birth has maintained a large programme stock and buys-in almost as much programming as it commissions (in 1985/86, 1768 hours of bought-in material versus 2145 hours of commissioned material, including repeats). It is against this background that Channel Four's undoubted success in restricting programme costs should be viewed.

CHAPTER THREE

The Internationalization of the Television Programme Market

Internationalization of information markets is far from a new phenomenon. The communications industries we know as the mass media owe their existence to the economies of scale that different technologies of reproduction and distribution have brought to the marketing of information. To realize the potential economies of scale markets must be extended in time or space or, preferably, both.

Gutenberg's development of printing with movable types rapidly conjured into existence a European market for printed books stretching from Riga to Naples and beyond. But in recent years a pervasive alarm at the dissolution of national cultural and communication unities has taken television as its stimulus, and 'wall-to-wall *Dallas*' is now an accepted shorthand for the baleful results attributed to this process. Internationalization of television is nothing new, though a long-standing flow of television across national borders has been amplified by technological change. The 'coca-cola' satellites 'attacking our artistic and cultural integrity', as Jack Lang the former French Minister of Culture put it (*The Financial Times*, 30 April 1984, p. 3), are prefigured in the customary prominence in the prime-time schedules of UK (and other national) television of imported programming. The BBC used thirty-five Canadian television dramas in the late-1950s in order to win back audiences it had lost to ITV and its 1984 screening of *The Thorn Birds* (a US mini-series) was used by the Corporation to boost its ratings (the screening of the eighth and final episode achieved for the BBC its biggest audience for more than two years).

A distinctive feature of the international information trade is its dual impact in the economic and cultural spheres. Thus to establish (if it could be established) that economic welfare was maximized by a division of labour and the international trade in television programmes is not sufficient to challenge those objections to such trades and specializations which are based on a negative assessment of the cultural impact of consumption of foreign television. We therefore consider below the economic and cultural dimensions of these trades separately.

Economic Advantage

The classical paradigm employed in trade theory is that of the international division of labour on the basis of absolute and comparative advantage. Aggregate welfare is maximized if countries *A* and *B* specialize in producing what each of them does best (where their absolute advantage lies) and trade with each other in order to secure supply of the whole range of products produced between them. Thus *A* might produce steel and *B* shoes. There will be international trade in shoes and steel. This holds if *A* is a superior producer of shoes and steel than *B*. It is still advantageous for *A* to secure shoes from *B* rather than produce them itself because production of shoes by *A* will consume resources (capital, labour etc.) that could generate a higher return if allocated to steel production. There are gains to be made from trade by specializing in your comparative advantage. To take an extreme instance, it would be possible to grow coffee in Scotland, and farm sheep in Brazil, but the resources consumed in heating Scottish glasshouses and clearing Brazilian pastures would be wasted for Scotland could successfully supply Brazil with lamb and Brazil could supply Scotland with coffee. Scotland has an absolute advantage in sheep and Brazil one in coffee. But where country *A* is better (i.e. more output for the same inputs) in production of both goods, the case for specialization still holds. For example, an accountant may be a brilliant and accurate typist yet it is still worthwhile for him or her to employ a secretary. The hourly income from the accounting profession is much more than either the cost of employing a secretary or the potential hourly income from typing. Specialization takes place in activities of comparative advantage.

Trade models are based on these notions of absolute and comparative advantage and are derived from David Ricardo and agricultural issues. Noticeably the bases of these advantages are the attributes of soil fertility and climate, that is, immobile factors. The model is widely applied to agricultural and industrial producers, but its relevance to the tertiary sector is less robust because the major factors of production required are internationally mobile.

International flows in television programmes are unequal and dominated by exports from the United States and, some way behind, the United Kingdom (Nordenstreng and Varis, 1974; Varis 1974, 1984). Whence comes this pre-eminence? It could be because of comparative advantage. If so, what are the factors exclusively or pre-eminently possessed by the UK and the US, and are they actually or potentially contestable by other producers? And under what conditions could the pre-eminence of the US and the UK be successfully challenged? Among the pertinent factors that contribute to the success of the US and UK in the international trade in television programmes are language (English being the most 'international' of world languages), the size and structure of domestic markets, the possession of a creative 'critical mass' of personnel competent in acting, make-up, videotape editing, and an infrastructure of prop, set and costume renters and makers. There is also a ready availability of financial services such as insurance, of manufacturers of electronic and cinematographic equipment, of processing laboratories and electronic services such as video standard conversion and image manipulation. Some of these — such as language — are geographically specific and could be defined as attributes of a classical comparative advantage; others, such as the availability of a pool of actors and efficient financial services are probably better defined as competitive advantages. However, for most purposes such distinctions are more theoretical than real. In production centres such as New York, Los Angeles and London there are factors of production which would require enormous and comprehensive investment to create elsewhere. Such investments have been applied in a variety of locations in order to establish national production industries.

State Support

In the Anglophone world the governments of Canada, Australia, New Zealand and Ireland have all applied substantial resources in direct subsidy or tax relief in order to establish and develop their domestic programme-production industries. Often this policy has been supported by import controls — the application of quotas, for instance. Their effect is to deny consumers foreign products that they would otherwise have consumed because of their superior price or performance characteristics relative to domestically produced products. The economic rationale — and it is important to recognize that the economic rationale is not the only one — for such policies is to establish an inant industry which will, when mature, be able to compete internationally unprotected by subsidy or quota and make a return to investors, whether directly or through fiscal contributions or both. Such policies do not seem to have been particularly successful. Hoskins and McFadyen (1986) have described the operation of Canada's national television programme-production policy which principally consists of a subsidy of 49 percent of the costs of qualifying productions. They cite the judgement of the government of Canada's Nielsen report (1986) that public support has 'only a modest impact on income, tax revenue productivity and the balance of payments'; and that 'although the economic benefits may exist, they are unlikely to be as high as for other economic investments'.

There are then two possible rationales for the subsidy policy — that there are positive externalities to be realized (i.e. indirect benefits) and that it is worth protecting an infant industry which, when established, will be internationally competitive. However, the infant-industry rationale is one that applies only to a temporary subsidy. If long-term or permanent subsidies are maintained, they can only be justified if they deliver the positive externalities, the economic, social or cultural benefits that would not otherwise be enjoyed.

Canadian experience suggests that the infant-industry strategy has failed because from a private calculus returns are not attractive enough to nationally or internationally mobile capital. Consequently, the indirect benefits, largely in the cultural and social areas, are the decisive rationale for subsidies of TV programme production in Canada.

The lack of success in establishing competitive suppliers of television programming outside the UK and USA can be explained in a variety of ways. The UK and US markets are the world's largest Anglophone markets. Each is resistant to penetration by imported television programmes (the UK because of regulation, the US because of the perception by broadcasters that audiences are uninterested in foreign programmes). UK and US producers are therefore able to recoup much, if not all, of their production costs in their home markets and to sell into foreign markets confident that however low the price secured from a programme sale the marginal cost of production (little more than the cost of an extra film print or videotape) will be amply exceeded. Nevertheless, the rising cost of TV programming is encouraging international co-productions which both spread costs and guarantee market access. Economies of scope are also available to UK and US producers because the same factors of production can be applied to different kinds of programme product. This reinforces their competitive advantage.

Towards Trade

Given the advantages of the dominant producers and their potential for charging near to marginal costs for exported material, it is rational for other countries to import acceptable programmes that are available at prices substantially below the costs of indigenous products. Since television programmes are relatively imperishable and not exhausted in consumption, consumers across the world are able to benefit from the low marginal cost of production and enjoy cheap, high-budget products from the existing dominant producers.

The US and UK are dominant but not omnipotent; there are important niches in the international market where they have no presence or a weak presence. Japan has been able to successfully occupy one such niche by producing computerized animations (mostly for children), and others exist. (A BBC source stated that there is a world undersupply of live-action, location-based dramas for children.) And there is a demand for programming in languages other than English that cannot be met by Anglophone producers (even in dubbed or subtitled form), and that reflects the experience of regions and cultures other than those of the North Atlantic. Mexico, for example, has been able to establish itself as an important regional and Spanish-language producer in spite of its physical and cultural proximity to the United States.

Looking strictly at the economic arguments, there is a very strong case for importing TV material from the dominant producers. If they pay low prices approaching marginal costs, the domestic resources that importing countries exchange for TV programmes are also of low cost. This assumes that importing countries have their own specialisms which they can develop and trade independently. Problems could possibly arise when control of domestic capital and productive capacity lies outside the country so that there is a leakage of income and a loss of sovereignty. Standard economic analysis emphasizes the international division of labour by the invisible hand. But increasingly the reality is the international division and distribution of capital between countries by multinational corporations.

Abstracting from these conditions, it is very unlikely that any country would independently decide to concentrate on a very limited range of trade goods where their comparative advantage lies. In these circumstances the performance of the economy is strongly influenced by price fluctuations of the specialism on international markets. The experiences of some countries specializing in commodities like coffee, sugar or oil which go from boom to bust, credit to massive debt are enough to warn many from the path of development indicated by trade theory. But TV material is not just an economic good; it is also a matter of culture.

Economy versus Culture

We turn now to those variables that are as significant structuring features of the international trade in television programmes as the economic factors considered above. Everywhere political institutions exist to realize benefits for those who control them. Benefits may be maximized in a particular location or for a particular group by distorting the processes of competition. The presence within the UK of television production facilities in Carlisle, Cardiff and the Channel Islands follows the imperatives of politics and not economics, for these facilities bring employment and other benefits such as augmented local patriotism because of the decision of broadcasting regulators to establish production in those provincial centres. Doubtless, if provincial production were not required by the IBA, the supply of programmes would be wholly from London at a lower overall cost but with the benefits disproportionately concentrated in London.

A particularly strong imperative that militates against the international organization of television production on a basis of comparative advantage and free trade is concern among non-Anglophones for the survival of their languages. This concern is particularly marked among, though not peculiar to, Francophones, and a major initiative known as 'La Francophonie' was launched by the Mitterrand socialist government to consolidate the French-language community around the world. Yet within the French language community there are complaints from the smaller nations that France has created a less than perfectly competitive regime. The survival of such national languages is a powerful reason adduced by governments for promoting indigenous production and restricting consumption of programmes in other languages.

Finally, there are cultural, moral and religious criteria exercised for the promotion of indigenous production and the restriction of consumption of foreign programmes. The impact of western culture on other societies is often disturbing. The cultural, moral and religious alarm at the consumption of international television programming is a conservative alarm based on the notion that imported values will have a deleterious effect on national mores. It seems very unlikely that the effect of foreign television will invariably be either negative or positive. In any case, maintenance of national sovereignty and identity are becoming increasingly difficult as the unities of economic and cultural production and consumption become increasingly transnational. And it is an open question whether the reharmonization of political, economic and cultural institutions — if it is to be sought and performed at all — should be performed by a more insistent nationalization of the economic and the cultural or by an internationalization of the political. At the micro level there are many cases in which the freedom, welfare and contentment of individuals are sustained and extended by the contestation of the authority and hegemony of the nation-state and the national culture.

The threat to communications sovereignty latent since the beginning of the twentieth century has, with the triple impact of new distribution technologies, new ideologies of deregulation and the accelerating demand for quantities of high-budget but low-cost software, become a matter of general concern. Moreover, the critique of the loss of communications sovereignty customarily runs in harness with a qualitative judgement that the new order and its product are inferior to the old. The concept of cultural imperialism is dependent on qualitative and quantitative judgements. The conditions of quantitative subordination are economic and organizational, the conditions of qualitative subordination are cultural and aesthetic.

It is an enduring European trait to hold up a mirror to US chauvinism. In the UK critical concern focuses on the proliferation of US-style hamburger outlets, not on the proliferation of Turkish, Greek and Lebanese kebab houses, or French, Italian, Indian and Chinese restaurants. The productivity of US cultural influences is very quickly forgotten — take, for example, the appropriation of its practices by modernist artists (e.g. Brecht and Grosz), the impact of Hollywood cinema on the 'Nouvelle Vague', the New German Cinema, or on Italian film-makers like Sergio Leone or, as has recently been claimed, Gianni Amelio.

The shift in film and television production from an artisanal mode of production where products are strongly marked by an authorial signature, whether that of director or scriptwriter, to series production in which it hardly makes sense to ask who is the author of *Dallas* or *Coronation Street*, is customarily deplored as a particularly insidious form of cultural imperialism. Yet this seems no more cultural imperialism than the adoption in Britain of the electrical engineering manufacturing techniques of Halske and Siemens, Pascalian mathematics or the astronomical theories of Copernicus and Galileo. The production techniques of US television series have dominated television in Britain since the 1960s, co-existing with (some would claim making possible) British television's substantial dominance of the UK audience ratings. It is this format that broadcast media have uniquely made possible and conjured into existence.

Consumer Demand and Trade

Radio and television's creation of an audience consuming upwards of four hours of broadcasting per day and a 'flow' of programming makes possible and demands long-running fictions in a way that neither the newspapers nor the cinema did. Cultural forms like *Coronation Street* and *Doctor Who* have endured in the UK for more than twenty years. What literary or dramatic precedents are there for narratives that exist without closure for so long? It is this shift in programme form, the demand from audiences for choice and high-budget productions, that has created an international market-place for products like *Dallas*. US producers, though paramount in this international market-place, are not the only players. A condition of consistent success in the international market is the production of programmes that appeal to international tastes and with a national content that is confined to the internationally current stereotypes of individual national histories and formations. Thus British television presents to the world a costumed image of Britain as a rigidly but harmoniously hierarchized class society in, for instance, *Brideshead Revisited, The Six Wives of Henry VIII* and *Upstairs, Downstairs*. Japan presents the shogun and samurai pasts and Italy *The Borgias*. And *Dallas, Dynasty, Hotel* and *Flamingo Road* represent the United States to international television viewers in terms of contemporary melodrama in which the values of capitalist business and the family are shown both positively and negatively.

The Trade Complex

It is in this complex ensemble of political, cultural and economic forces that the international trade in television programmes is caught. None of the forces in play operate singly. The low marginal cost of production of television programmes will tend to call into existence markets that are widely extended in time and space. Political and cultural forces for the preservation of national language and culture will tend to inhibit these kinds of extension. This ensemble of forces has been imperfectly understood largely in terms of two contradictory paradigms: those of media imperialism and international division of labour on the basis of comparative advantage. Neither paradigm is adequate. The comparative-advantage paradigm is questionable in its economic analysis and for its neglect of political, linguistic and cultural criteria. The media-imperialism paradigm is weakened by its lack of recognition that imported programmes may be important sources of diversity and quality in television programme schedules. Also its central thesis that 'most countries are passive recipients of information' (Varis, 1984: 152) is a contention that is hard to reconcile with the evidence of Katz and Liebes (1985) that different national and ethnic groups make highly differentiated use of that quintessentially international programme *Dallas*.

We do not, therefore, offer the study which follows as a definitive analysis, but we hope that we have contributed useful data to a field of study that has long been strong in polemic but weak in facts. We believe too that the heuristic paradigms that have been used to understand the international trade in television have been insufficiently attentive to the special economic characteristics of an information commodity which poses, along with its non-economic characteristics, peculiar problems. The imperishability and inexhaustibility in consumption of this information commodity structure international information trades.

The imperishability of the information commodity means that new products have to compete in the market with old ones. With each generation, new cohorts of potential consumers for Chaplin films, more than 300 episodes of $M*A*S*H*$, and Disney animations enter the market as consumers. Their attention and market power are fragmented among an ever-increasing range of choices. The owners of 'old' intellectual properties (e.g. Disney) can, with judicious exploitation of their products, present formidable barriers to the entry of new products. The new products have to return their costs (at least) to investors; old products have often fully amortized their costs in previous and less-competitive markets. But 'new' products that enjoy early and secure entry to large and affluent markets (which may be partially closed by regulation, oligopolistic structure or the chauvinism of consumers) may amortize costs in primary markets and be available for exploitation at 'dumping' prices (when only marginal costs require to be recovered) in secondary markets.

Historically these characteristics of the information commodity (and markets) have favoured *producers* in the United States. When non-US producers are unprotected by regulation, oligopoly or the resistance of consumers to American values, language and products, they have tended to be defeated in competition with US producers. But there is evidence that markets are unable to satisfy consumers' demand for certain cultural and information goods because of the action of national governments. The unsatisfied demand may be for cheaper goods than national producers can offer or for distinctive cultural goods that national producers are unable or unwilling to supply. Indeed imports are often not supplied because of a perception that national identity itself will be compromised by increased consumption of foreign information goods. But strong though the national forces are, the internationalization of information markets is growing and classes of goods are coming into existence which have fewer and fewer national characteristics. This is, of course, a phenomenon that can be positively or negatively evaluated, but those for and against these changes share a view that the dislocation between international unities of production and consumption (the economic and the cultural) and the national political unity of the nation-state is increasing.

The UK's place in these processes is contradictory and little understood. The transnational cultural and economic unity that UK information producers have customarily inhabited is that of the international Anglophone (predominantly North Atlantic) community. But since the UK's accession to the European Economic Community the *political* unity it inhabits has become increasingly European. This pressure for unity is starting to Europeanize the cultural and economic activities of the UK (and other member states) in the information sector (see Commission of the European Communities, 1984). In a plethora of instances the UK is having to choose Atlanticist or European solutions (e.g. Westland, Ford's bid to purchase Austin Rover, British Telecom's acquisition of Mitel).

Ravault (1980) has pointed out how imperfect the linkages are between cultural production and consumption and trade and other political and economic forces. He pertinently contrasts the success of the US and UK in international media markets with the decline in their political, economic and military power, and observes that West Germany among other states successfully reconciles importation of information goods with increased power in other arenas.

There is, then, no stable interpretative paradigm available which can act as an initial guiding hypothesis. The evidence of international trade in television programmes can only with selective application be made to fit available paradigms. Our view is that existing relations are highly context-dependent and that market structures — rapidly changing in an international broadcasting order where new technologies and ideologies are exercising their power — are the most important determinants of international information flows.

The television-programme production industry in the UK has reached a stable *modus vivendi* with other forces in the international market-place. This could not have been anticipated given the vulnerability of UK film producers to competition from the United States. The factors that give the US movie majors dominance remain — a shared language, US economic power and ability to amortize high production costs in the domestic market, and the fundamental attractiveness of the US product to audiences. But the vertical integration of producers and distributors in television, the successful imposition of quota restrictions on imports, the limitation of distribution capacity (all functions of state regulation) have enforced a different regime in television. These conditions of television programme production in the UK are all changing as national communications sovereignty declines. But changes in the market structure of UK trade partners — notably the United States — mean that their producers are also vulnerable to competition in the new television order. The decline in advertising revenue and network audience share create in the United States conditions more favourable to import penetration and less favourable to high-budget domestic production than before.

We describe below the nature of UK television programme trades, the structure of the UK market and the regulatory and other forces that are in play seeking variously to maintain or change the existing order. It seems that British television producers (though perhaps not consumers) have the opportunity to make history more on the terms of their own choosing than did their antecedents in the era of film. The following presents our best attempt to provide data and analysis of the trade in TV programming.

British Programme Trades

The OECD estimates that the OECD volume of audio-visual production is about $26 billion (of which almost half is earned by United States firms). Of this total no more than $1 billion is traded internationally and of that $400 million is TV programmes and videofilms. In 1980, $350 million of trade in telefilms emanated from the United States with the United Kingdom, the second biggest exporter, exporting $22 million in telefims (OECD, 1986: 23, 25).

However, the Department of Trade and Industry (DTI) publication *British Business* states the overseas receipts of the BBC and IBA programme contractors in 1980 to be $50 million (*British Business*, 19 September 1986, p. 42). Although a comparison of DTI and OECD figures is not a comparison of like with like (for the DTI figures embrace world trades denominated in sterling and the OECD only OECD trades in US dollars), there is an uncomfortably large discrepancy between them. This discrepancy is symptomatic of the uncertainty of the data available on these trades and trade in the information sector generally. But though it is difficult to establish the volume of trades authoritatively, there is no reason to doubt the OECD's definition of United States domination of international markets and the United Kingdom's second place.

In a survey of services in the UK economy, the *Bank of England Quarterly* comments that

> earnings from film and television amounted to 2.8% of exports and 3.5% of imports of financial and 'other' services in 1984 and showed a surplus of £131m. Real growth in this sector has been strong but somewhat erratic, in recent years. (Bank of England, 1985: 413)

The exports, imports and the real balance of trade are shown in Figure 3.1. It is important to note that the *Bank of England Quarterly* does not disaggregate films and television. There are difficulties in doing so — many programmes produced and traded internationally for exhibition on television are recorded on film and may also be exhibited theatrically. Similarly, films may be distributed on video-cassettes and be consumed through exhibition on a domestic television set whether the signal originates from a terrestrial or satellite broadcast, from cable or from a domestic video-cassette recorder.

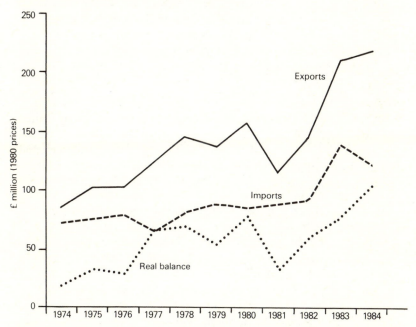

Figure 3.1   *Films and Television: UK Service Earnings and Payments (Bank of England, 1985)*

The bases of this analysis are formed by *British Business*, which reports annually on overseas transactions in films and television material (and it is on *British Business*'s surveys that the Bank of England's analysis is based), and the annual reports and accounts of the largest British television production companies (the ITCA member companies, the BBC and others such as Sianel Pedwar Cymru (S4C)). This information from the public domain has been supplemented by information of uncertain reliability from trade journals and by personal interviews with industry representatives. There are important contradictions within and between these information sources. For example, the table 'Overseas transactions of the BBC and IBA programme contractors' published regularly in *British Business* cannot be reconciled with the reports on overseas sales in company accounts. And a telephone enquiry to *British Business* (9 January 1986) elicited the information that *British Business* had mistakenly classified TV material under film in their analysis since it originated from television production companies which had 'film' as part of the company name. There are further difficulties in the inconsistent way in which companies report trades by time (calendar or financial years or individual company accounting years) and by place (one company's residual category 'rest of the world' may include territories differentiated and specified in another company's accounts).

There are further difficulties in that material may be acquired through exchange or barter and similar products may in different years move between traded and non-traded categories. The difference between a co-production and a pre-sale is often only semantic, but a co-production is probably not recorded in trade statistics whereas a pre-sale usually is.

The last eight years (to 1985) have seen an increased volume of trade between the UK and the rest of the world in television programmes (Table 3.1). Both imports and exports of programmes have grown, though imports have (particularly in the last five years) tended to grow more rapidly than exports. In the period between 1976 and 1980 the average positive trade balance in television programmes was £12 million pounds per annum. Since 1980 the positive balance of trade has declined, although in 1985 a very strong positive balance of trade was re-established (of £28 million).

In the period between 1968 and 1976 receipts from the trade in television programmes more than trebled, from £5 million to £18 million; and doubled (from £18 million to £36 million) between 1976 and 1977. Expenditure on overseas programming more than quadrupled between 1968 and 1976, from £4 million to £18 million, fell

Table 3.1 *Receipts of the BBC and IBA Programme Contractors, 1978–85: Analysis by Area (£ million)*

	EEC	Other W. European Countries	USA and Canada	Other Developed Countries[a]	Rest of World	Total	US and Canadian Share (%)	Balance of Trade[b]
1978	6	3	17	6	5	37	46	15
1979	10	4	18	7	3	42	43	14
1980	8	3	30	6	3	50	60	19
1981	10	4	21	8	4	47	45	10
1982	11	3	35	9	5	63	56	8
1983	11	2	47	11	6	77	61	8
1984	15	4	51	14	7	91	56	1
1985	14	6	65	16	9	110	59	28

[a] Other developed countries are Australia, New Zealand, Japan and South Africa.
[b] Receipts less expenditure.

slightly in 1977, and grew at an increasing rate to the mid-1980s and then fell in 1985. Movements in the volume of trade are not regular either on a year-to-year basis or in terms of the geographical area in which the trading partner is located.

However, it is clear that North America (of which the United States is the main market component with about ten times the population of Canada) is by far the most important single market. It accounts for between 43 percent (1979) and 61 percent (1983) of the export market for British television programmes and between 43 percent (1977) and 71 percent (1984) of the imports of programming into the UK by value. The substantial improvement in the balance of trade in 1985 was principally due to increased receipts and decreased expenditure in North America (see Table 3.2).

BBC Television Programme Exports
BBC Enterprises is the subsidiary through which the BBC sells programmes (and exploits other assets such as the BBC Micro computer). BBC Enterprises' exports rose between 1978 and 1982, dipped in 1982/83 and continued to rise in 1983/84. BBC Enterprises disaggregates the North American market into the United States and Canada, though in contrast to the figures cited in Tables 3.1 and 3.2, which aggregate all British trades, the North American market is less important than the European market for the BBC (except in the years 1978/79 and 1981/82). The growth in the sales of BBC Enterprises has been principally in the three major markets of Australia, the United States and Europe (see Table 3.3). There has also been significant

recent growth in BBC sales to South America which follows the BBC use of Mexico as a centre for dubbing its programmes into Spanish. BBC Enterprises has withdrawn from a number of markets (notably in the Middle East) because of non-payment by customers.

Table 3.2   *Expenditure of the BBC and IBA Programme Contractors, 1978–85: Analysis by Area (£ million)*

	EEC	Other W. European Countries	USA and Canada	Other Developed Countries[a]	Rest of World	Total	US and Canadian Share (%)
1978	4	2	12	1	3	22	55
1979	6	2	15	1	4	28	54
1980	5	4	18	1	3	31	58
1981	11	2	19	1	4	37	51
1982	9	4	36	1	5	55	65
1983	12	4	47	1	5	69	68
1984	16	3	64	2	5	90	71
1985	13	4	56	4	5	82	68

[a] Other developed countries are Australia, New Zealand, Japan and South Africa.

Source: figures taken from *British Business* dated 16 September 1983, 5 October 1984, 30 August–5 September 1985, 19 September 1986.

Table 3.3   *BBC Enterprises Foreign Programme Sales 1978/79 to 1983/84 (£ million)*

	Year to 31 March					
	1979	1980	1981	1982	1983	1984
Europe	2.2	2.5	2.9	3.6	3.5	5.7
USA	1.8	1.6	2.0	5.6	2.5	4.3
Australasia	1.6	2.4	2.2	3.3	3.1	3.9
Mid/Far East	1.0	0.9	1.0	1.6	1.0	0.4
Canada	0.6	0.5	0.5	0.5	0.7	0.5
South America[a]	—	—	—	—	0.7	1.0
Other	0.4	0.6	1.1	1.1	0.9	1.6
Total	7.6	8.5	9.7	15.7	12.4	17.4
UK	0.6	0.4	0.5	1.1	0.5	0.6
Co-producers contributions to programme production	5.5	2.9	2.7	4.6	4.6	5.9
Merchandizing: library sales exhibitions, BBC records etc. (including UK)[b]	1.6	3.1	4.8	6.7	12.8	13.4
Total	9.8	12.0	15.0	22.9	25.7	31.4

[a] No specific breakdown of South America figures pre-1982/83.

[b] Merchandizing figure includes BBC Micro computers from 1982/83 onwards.

Source: BBC Television Facts and Figures, 1980–85.

ITCA Companies' Exports

From 1978 to 1983 ITCA exports grew steadily (though with a decline in 1981) with increased exports to the United States accounting for most of the growth in sales (see Table 3.4). The analysis of the activities of individual ITCA members is hampered by the paucity and contradictory nature of the information in the public domain (chiefly company annual reports and accounts and the annual DTI summary report in *British Business*), and the disinclination of representatives of the companies engaged in the trade in television programmes to specify volume or value of trades. However, it is clear that the largest companies of the British independent television system (Central, Granada, London Weekend, Thames) are the most vigorous exporters.

Table 3.4   *ITCA Companies' North American Export Figures 1978–83 (£ million)*

	Total ITCA Company Export Sales	ITCA Sales to N. America	% of ITCA Companies' Sales to N. America
1978	29.5	14.4	49.0
1979	33.5	15.9	47.5
1980	40.0	27.5	68.8
1981	31.5	14.9	47.3
1982	50.5	31.8	63.0
1983	59.5	42.2	70.9

The figures for the volume of ITCA companies' export sales are calculated by subtracting the annual BBCtv export figures (as stated in *BBC Television Facts and Figures*, 1980–85) from the total figures for the overseas transactions of the BBC and IBA programme contractors, as stated in the DTI publication *British Business* 1983, 1984 and 1985.

Thames Television, the largest of the ITCA member companies, has been second only to the BBC in foreign programme sales. The BBC draws on programming for two channels while Thames produces only for its franchise area, London during the week (Monday until Friday 5.45 p.m.) (though many Thames programmes are nationally networked). In all the tables which follow the year is the period ending 31 March and the amounts are £ thousand. Thames Television's receipts from overseas sales between 1980 and 1985 (excluding format sales) were:

1980	1981	1982	1983	1984	1985
4,748	9,783	11,802	13,108	13,475	19,253

Source: Thames Television's report and and accounts.

Other ITCA member companies have similarly increased the value of their sales of programming overseas. Granada TV International's receipts from overseas sales were:

1980	1981	1982	1983	1984
n.r.	n.r.	2,280	4,320	6,330

Source: Granada TV International's report and accounts.

London Weekend Television's receipts from overseas sales were:

1980	1981	1982	1983	1984
n.r.	n.r.	n.r.	3,010	6,390

Source: LWT's report and accounts.

Yorkshire TV Enterprises receipts from overseas programme sales were:

1980	1981	1982	1983	1984
n.r.	n.r.	90	560	1,000

Source: Yorkshire TV Enterprises' report and accounts.

Smaller ITCA member companies vary greatly in their overseas sales. Border Television records no overseas programme sales, but Anglia and HTV have enjoyed success. HTV's overseas programme sales were:

1980	1981	1982	1983	1984
n.r.	n.r.	162	1,069	3,095

Source: HTV's report and accounts.

Anglia TV's overseas programme sales were:

1980	1981	1982	1983	1984
n.r.	n.r.	435	262	676

Source: Anglia TV's report and accounts.

However, Anglia TV's unremarkable performance is improved when the performance of its subsidiary Survival Anglia Ltd (of which the parent company owns an 81 percent share) is considered:

1980	1981	1982	1983	1984
n.r.	n.r.	1,639	931	1,631

Source: ibid.

The achievement of Anglia TV exemplifies two characteristic patterns in British TV programme producers' overseas programme trades —

that of exploiting a niche market, and that of exploiting markets through subsidiaries. Thames Television principally conducts its overseas programme sales through Thames Television International and Granada through Granada TV International.

British Television Companies and Foreign Co-Productions

Direct programme sales to overseas markets are not the only form of trading or production relation between British television companies and overseas markets. There are a variety of co-productions concluded either under co-production treaties whereby the programme or series produced counts as a domestic product in the home market of each co-production partner, or in a less formal arrangement such as that between BBC's *Horizon* documentary programme and the equivalent *Nova* series produced by WGBH in Boston for PBS in the United States. The arrangement is one in which the BBC and WGBH exchange a number of programmes each year. Co-producers' contributions to BBC programme production is stated as (in £ million):

1978/79	1979/80	1980/81	1981/82	1982/83	1983/84
5.5	2.9	2.7	4.6	4.6	5.9

Source: BBC Television Facts and Figures, 1980–85.

The production of Central TV's *Kennedy*, LWT's *Dempsey and Makepeace* and Thames Television's *Reilly: Ace of Spies* were all done on the basis of a pre-sale agreement with a United States client. *Reilly* had, for British television, a high production budget of £4.5 million (eleven episodes of 52 minutes, one of 75 minutes), i.e. about £370,000 per programme hour. And this exceptional commitment (which required authorization by the main board of Thames Television) was made possible by a pre-sale agreement with Mobil Oil of $100,000 per programme hour. *Dempsey and Makepeace* was pre-sold to the *Chicago Tribune* group for an estimated $100,000 to $200,000 per programme hour (*The Sunday Times*, 20 January 1985, p. 38). An interview with Herb Schmeiz, the Vice President of Mobil Oil responsible for Mobil Oil's sponsorship of PBS television drama (by R. Collins, 14.2.85), established an average range of between $100,000 and $200,000 per programme hour as the acquisition cost of 'quality' television drama for exhibition on PBS.

The term 'co-production' describes a wide range of collaborative activities concerned with the finance and actual production of television material. Rarely do co-productions involve a fifty-fifty share of funding, production and distribution responsibilities between partners. Most co-productions represent the collaboration of a project-initiating company with a funding and/or facilities partner. In addition, the nature of such financial collaboration is such that there is an increasing 'blurring' of the boundaries of co-production and pre-sales activities.

BBC Co-Productions

The BBC has a long-established tradition of co-production activities, particularly with the (Anglophone) Commonwealth. Such co-productions have typically concerned programmes of the documentary, wildlife, travelogue, cultural and on-location historical drama variety. In such productions the BBC has traditionally been both the dominant partner in creative terms and usually the sole beneficiary of subsequent international programme sales (see Table 3.5).

Table 3.5   *BBC Enterprises: Co-Producers' Contributions to Programme Production/Foreign Programme Sales (£ million)*

Year to 31 March	Co-Productions	Foreign Sales Contributions
1979	5.5	7.6
1980	2.9	8.5
1981	2.7	9.7
1982	4.6	15.7
1983	4.6	12.4
1984	5.9	17.4

Foreign sales figures include programme pre-sales income.
Source: BBC Television Facts and Figures, 1980–85.

For programmes not simply requiring a specific foreign setting and/or screen talent, co-production partners are sought for purely financial purposes. Co-production finance is looked for firstly from BBC Enterprises, then by international shopping around. Byron Parkin (Deputy Managing Director of BBC Enterprises) outlined the process as follows:

> When programmes are offered to the controllers of BBC1 and BBC2, often they don't have sufficient money to take the more prestigious ones and so they tell the producers that the balance will have to be found from outside co-producing partners. The co-production department makes a list of all those programmes looking for co-production money and their first port of call is Enterprises. We say we'll put so much into that one and so on. After they've had our answer they go round the world trying to find the

outstanding sums. For *The Living Planet* we put a substantial amount of money in and then we went out to try to pre-sell it. All of that pre-sale money comes back to us. On big productions pre-selling is very important and necessary to re-coup the large amounts of up-front money. It's a growing trend. (Wade, 1985: 45)

As Parkin describes the relationship, foreign co-production partners are passive providers of finance to the BBC. Research interviews and reports in the trade press do, however, indicate a growing resistance to this approach on the part of foreign television companies (particularly given the increasing range of players in this area). Inta Janovskis (Director of Programme Development, Canadian Broadcasting Corporation) singled out the lack of production consultation and zero profit-share in subsequent sales in particular as major shortcomings in BBC co-production deals. If this resistance becomes more pronounced it seems likely that the BBC will look to more 'co-production' deals with non-producing TV operations such as the American Worldwide Holding Corporation (a US syndication company), where the 'co-pro' arrangement is effectively a high-price pre-sale which gives the US co-producer rights to US syndication.

In the area of high-budget drama production the BBC has altered its traditional approach to co-productions. The case of *Tender is the Night* in particular illustrates how the high production cost of prestige drama increasingly requires the BBC to take major co-production partners who have a significant role in both funding and creative decision-making. The success of the BBC/Showtime Scott Fitzgerald mini-series looks likely to act as a model for future high-budget productions, though details of the allocation of subsequent sales rights have not been made available.

Channel Four's European Co-Productions
Joint productions with European partners have been an established aspect of British television co-production activities for some time, but recent developments have led to increased activity of this kind. The significant factor has been the introduction of Channel Four with its specific cultural programming brief. The similarity of its programming policies to other European broadcasters such as Zweites Deutsches Fernsehen's (ZDF's) *Das Kleine Fernsehspiel* in West Germany has been an obvious incentive to co-production.

Channel Four has actively pursued European co-productions since its introduction in 1982 (e.g. its £1 million input into the Channel Four/RTE/Astramead series *The Price*). In addition to collaboration in TV drama co-production, a second area of co-production is coming to assume increasing prominence, that of cultural, documentary and TV feature-film co-productions involving a number of European partners (though it should be noted that only one or two of the partners involved in such multi-partner co-productions usually control production decisions — the others characteristically provide 'pre-sale' type finance).

Justin Dukes (Managing Director, Channel Four) has emphasized the potential long-term importance of European co-productions to minimize the duplication of European production around common European interests (e.g. cultural anniversaries, performance events etc.). He has also predicted that up to 15 percent of future Channel Four production could derive from such arrangements (thus freeing around 40 percent of the notional cost of a similar domestic production for other production activities).

Additional interest in the area of multi-partner European co-production has arisen from the publication of the EEC Commission's Green Paper *Television Without Frontiers* (Commission of the European Communities, 1984), and the ensuing debate. The European Broadcasting Union's (EBU) canvassing for a European production fund was one of the measures referred to in the Commission's Green Paper. It is significant, however, that (even given the acknowledged importance of such production activities) European broadcasters have largely rejected plans for the provision of an EEC-administered European co-production fund of $20 million. The BBC's observations are representative:

> The BBC is sceptical about the usefulness of a fund but it all depends on what it is for. In principle the BBC would oppose any initiative which brought Government or EEC involvement in editorial decisions. Co-production projects are already made in reasonable numbers in Europe and extra money alone is unlikely to significantly increase such co-productions. The BBC therefore would ask what purpose a fund might serve. (House of Lords, 1985: 70)

This rejection follows lengthy discussions between representatives of companies such as Channel Four, ZDF and Italy's RAI, and their reluctance to collaborate with a funding source which requires executive supervisory powers over productions funded by it.

ITCA Companies' Co-Productions
Though information on the annual income from ITCA company co-production deals is unavailable, reports in the trade press indicate that in addition to co-productions with European and Commonwealth

partners, the ITCA companies are attempting to increase and diversify their co-production activities with a range of US partners. There has also been greater willingness to work with foreign partners in a genuinely collaborative manner — the Yorkshire TV/Alan Landsburg co-production of *Glory Boys*, for example, was produced in separate versions for the UK and US markets (see *TV World*, August 1985, pp. 12–14).

Co-production deals encompass a wide range of financial arrangements and production responsibilities, and such arrangements often overlap with 'pre-sales' (i.e. the purchase of a product prior to its production or completion). The growing importance of such deals has led in some cases to the pre-sale purchaser being able to dictate script modifications and approve casting (e.g. LWT's *Dempsey and Makepeace* pre-sale deal with the *Chicago Tribune* group), and thereby to the production of ostensibly British domestic-market programming tailored to the American market.

The production and pre-sale of the programme material of British television companies specifically developed by independent agents for American network transmission also blurs the boundaries between co-production and pre-sale. HTV has been particularly active in this field, with a number of major deals with CBS and NBC. Deals such as that struck with CBS for the production of the TV film *Arch of Triumph* have seen the US partner supplying over 50 percent of the production budget via its pre-sale licence fee (and resulted in allegations from within the industry of HTV simply acting as a 'facilities house' for foreign production (see *Broadcast*, 20 April 1984, p. 48).

ITCA company subsidiaries such as Central's Zenith have also involved themselves in similar activities, co-producing properties specifically for the US market (e.g. the programme developed by MTM (Mary Tyler Moore productions) called *Finnegan Begin Again* which starred Mary Tyler Moore, was directed by Joan Micklin Silver, and shot entirely on location in the USA) which have been subsequently broadcast by the parent company in the UK. (Subsidiaries of ITCA companies such as Zenith and Euston Films have an advantage over ITCA parent companies in that their residuals are calculated on the anomalous basis of them being film production companies rather than television producers and are consequently smaller.) The question of residual payments to creative personnel following sale of a property in additional markets is an important influence on ITCA company strategy and has led to the anomalous situation of the BBC receiving a fee for the relay of its programmes by cable in Belgium and the ITCA companies declining to accept a fee because of their consequential liability to pay residuals.

Programme Format Sales

Thames Television has developed further methods of exploiting its intellectual property assets. *The Benny Hill Show*, a product that has enjoyed considerable longevity in Britain (and of which, therefore, there is an extensive archive) is re-edited into twenty-two half-minute units and sold to the US syndication market for 'stripping' (broadcasting in a regular slot over a long time). New *Benny Hill Specials* produced in and for the UK are sold to Home Box Office for its satellite/cable Pay TV service on an exclusive basis for eighteen months. The rights then revert to Thames Television, the shows are re-edited into a different time-format and are sold to the syndication market for stripping. The US syndication market demands high volumes of programmes so that a stable schedule can be constructed and audiences know that, for example, *M*A*S*H** will be screened at 7.00 p.m. on Thursday evenings. British programming is characteristically not made in sufficient volume for stripping in this way and however high the quality of individual programmes or short series their lack of volume makes them unattractive in the most important US markets. Thus a series such as *Fawlty Towers* made in a dozen episodes is attractive only to PBS in the United States.

Thames has developed further successful strategies for exploiting its intellectual property in the US television market and has sold a series of 'formats' to US producers. The original British situation comedies *Keep It in the Family, Man About the House, Robin's Nest* and *George and Mildred* have been transmuted for the US market into new sitcoms *Too Close for Comfort, Three's Company, Three's a Crowd* and *The Ropers*, which have enjoyed considerable success. *Three's Company* has been the most successful comedy in syndication, topping the sweeps in February, May, July, November 1984 and in February 1985. The success of the American-format clones has provoked Thames to sell the British original versions of the sitcoms to US broadcasters under the title *The Thames Comedy Originals*, which are advertised as: '156 half-hours for strong, cost effective stripping'. Thames has also established a Californian production company, Grand Central Productions, as a fifty-fifty joint venture with its long-standing US distributor, D. L. Taffner. Grand Central Productions proposes to make programmes for six principal US buyers — Home Box Office, Showtime, the syndication market and the commercial networks ABC, CBS and NBC. Thames's explicit equity stake in Grand Central Productions is a novel initiative in its North American operations which have customarily been through companies in which it takes no equity but a share of profit.

The Profitability of Overseas Sales

Sales to overseas markets are likely to continue as an important element of British television companies' activities. The BBC is unable to continue its existing activities and levels of employment at the current rate of its licence-fee revenue and is actively pursuing revenue-rising activities including publishing, the sale of information from its archive and a more vigorous exploitation of its programme stock by BBC Enterprises. The relationship between average and marginal costs in television programme production is such that sales of programmes to small overseas markets for low prices may still realize very high profits in relation to the costs incurred. A hypothetical example will clarify this argument. A programme may be produced at a cost of £200,000. Much, if not all, of this cost of production will be defrayed from revenues accruing in the UK home market (whether from the sale of audiences to advertisers or from licence-fee receipts). The cost of printing an extra copy of a film or dubbing an additional copy of the programme onto videotape is nugatory compared with the 'first-copy' costs against which all production costs (except those of making an additional copy, which is little more than the cost of a video-cassette or the charges of a film laboratory) may be allocated. Indeed, the customary practice of the ITCA companies is to write off costs in the UK.

Thames Television's formula (which appears in each annual *Report and Accounts*) is representative of the ITCA companies' practice: 'The cost of own productions and film rights is wholly written off on first transmission within the United Kingdom'.

To the marginal cost of making a second film or video-cassette for sale in additional markets must be added the costs of promotion, residual payments to actors and other personnel, marketing and sales. These may be considerable. In 1984 BBC Enterprises incurred the costs shown in Table 3.6. This generated a turnover of £31,414,923, and a pre-tax profit of £5,852,173.

However, it is likely that many of the costs incurred by BBC Enterprises do not vary proportionally with turnover, and profit will rise more than proportionally with each additional sale. Thus, even markets in which low returns are realized may — once 'first-copy' costs have been defrayed in the home market — be highly profitable.

Table 3.6   *BBC Enterprises Costs 1984*

Costs	(£)
Sales	13,715,986
Distribution	6,671,379
Administration	4,379,609
Interest	1,107,225
Total	25,834,199

Source: BBC Enterprises Report and Accounts 1984/85.

The United States Market

A consequence of the profitability of foreign sales of television programmes and the relatively uncompetitive nature of the domestic market (in which there is a very indirect relationship between consumption and audience size on the one hand and revenues and profitability on the other) is a tendency to tailor programming to the requirements of overseas markets; and in particular to the requirements of the largest and potentially most rewarding market of the United States. This tendency is, in the commercial sector, relatively satisfactorily controlled by regulation (though whether it should be an aim of regulators to control it or deny British audiences Americanized programmes for which a consistent liking has been demonstrated is another question). The IBA in 1981 declined to renew the franchise of ATV to transmit programmes and sell television advertising in the Midlands region of England. ATV had a long history of producing evidently 'mid-Atlantic' programming such as *Baron, The Protectors* and *Man in a Suitcase*. ATV's application for reappointment to the Midlands commercial TV franchise stated: 'The outstanding performance of the corporation as a dollar earner has led to three Queen's Awards for Exports, while two subsidiaries have also received individual awards for export achievement' (ATV, May 1980). And an interview with Chris Rowley (21 January 1986), then Chief Scheduling Officer of the IBA, revealed the willingness of the authority to make representations to programme companies which were deemed to be insufficiently attentive to the interests (as defined by the IBA) of the UK audience. Given the power of the IBA to withdraw franchises and the Authority's demonstrated preparedness to exercise its power (three important contractors — ATV, Southern Television and Westward Television — did not have their franchises renewed in 1981), it is unlikely that its sensitivity to 'mid-Atlantic' programming will be ignored. However, the pull of the United States market remains a potent one; the predominance of high-budget costume drama in the output of British companies is likely to be related to the evident PBS market for 'quality' television of this order.

But there are characteristics of the British and American markets that are difficult to reconcile. The United States market demands (outside PBS) a high volume of product for stripping. There are very few British programmes that meet this requirement (*Doctor Who* and *The Benny Hill Show* do and have been successfully sold to the US syndication market), though ATV with programmes such as *The Prisoner* and *The Muppet Show* attempted to develop British product in volumes suitable for stripping. Rather the programme form that is perhaps most successfully 'amphibious' in both markets is the mini-series. Much of the drama output sold to PBS for screening under Mobil Oil's sponsorship as *Masterpiece Theatre* or *Mystery!* has been of this kind and characteristically commands prices of between $100,000 and $200,000 per hour. Pre-sale agreements with Mobil enabled Thames Television to proceed with its expensive productions of *Rumple of the Bailey* and *Reilly: Ace of Spies*. (*Reilly* cost £4.5 million for 12¼ programme hours; revenue from the PBS pre-sale accounted for perhaps 20 percent — depending on how the dollar–pound parity is calculated — of its budget. The sale of Canadian Francophone rights — an audience of about eight million — realized $16,000 per hour for Thames.)

Such agreements have become of increasing importance to UK producers. Indeed Central TV's daughter company, Zenith (set up after the successful transnational mini-series production *Kennedy*) receives a maximum of 50 percent of its production budgets from the parent company. The requirements of the IBA and institutional *amour propre* are such that few UK producers will admit to any relationship with co-production partners other than British autonomy and control or to any tailoring of cast or productions to foreign markets. But the quantity of co-production and joint ventures and the importance of foreign markets is such that it is unimaginable that the anticipated requirements of the most important market, the USA, have no impact on editorial and creative decisions.

The joint-venture, co-production phenomenon is a two-way street. A number of US series owe their continued existence to their success in the UK market (*Fame* and *Cagney and Lacey*, for example), and Lawrence Gershman, President of the MGM/UA TV Group, testifies to the need of US producers for foreign partners and the power of co-producers:

What were co-financing deals in years past are now becoming fully fledged international co-productions today. The US and European partners involved are not only sharing production costs but more than that, there's a shared creative role in the project as well. At least for us it's no longer a case of a major studio saying to a foreign partner 'Give us your money but don't open your mouth'. The foreigners want to be part of the editorial creative process and on that side they're playing a greater role than ever before. (*TV World*, August 1985, p. 12)

To be sure, the two-way street carries a disproportionately high amount of heavy US traffic, but the flow *is* two-way. No market in the world can now consistently support the cost and volume of production necessary to supply its domestic market. The United States' long-standing comparative advantage in audio-visual media production has depended crucially on the size of its domestic market. The command of a high-income market of about 250 million people, in general resistant to import penetration, has enabled US film and TV producers to invest very large sums in production budgets, recoup these investments in the home market and sell very high quality product with high production values at marginal cost in foreign markets. In other commodity markets this behaviour would be described as 'dumping'. But 'dumping' is normative, not exceptional in information markets, and assuming that the United States succeeds in establishing that trade in services is within the purview of the new General Agreement on Tariffs and Trade (GATT), it is hard to see how a GATT agreement on services that deals satisfactorily with dumping will be reached.

Variety (5 October 1983, pp. 56, 57, 70, 71) estimates the production cost per episode of US TV series as follows:

Dynasty	$850,000
Hotel	$700,000
Dallas	$850,000
Falcon Crest	$750,000
Knots Landing	$650,000
St Elsewhere	$750,000

Producers have customarily been able to recoup these costs in the US market by licensing a network for two screenings of an hour of programming. However, this equilibrium is being disturbed as the production costs of US television series rise and the ability of broadcasters to pay declines. Broadcasters' ability to pay is declining as competition (most importantly with the challenge to the three networks' hegemony by the 'fourth network' Fox and independent stations grouping into syndicates) becomes more effective and as advertising revenue declines. The networks' prime-time share of the

US audience has declined to below 75 percent (from 90 percent at the beginning of the 1980s) and advertising revenues fell in 1985 by 2.6 percent. A prime-time slot 'that commanded over $100,000 two years ago is now selling for under $95,000' (*The Financial Times*, 12 September 1986, p. 24). A representative example of production-cost inflation is the US series *Miami Vice*. The two-hour pilot for *Miami Vice* cost $5 million (the norm is $3 million):

> To give the pilot the look of a feature film it was shot partially at night — which means paying technicians overtime. And there was no stinting on props. The undercover narcotics agent played by Don Johnson drives a $125,000 Ferrari Daytona, lives on a $150,000 Chris Craft offshore racer, has a pet alligator Elvis and wears designer suits. Says Mann [the producer] 'An undercover policeman making drug buys can't show up in ripped Levis.' (*Business Week*, 11 February 1985, p. 77)

Each episode of *Miami Vice* costs $1.2 million, of which $850,000 is covered by NBC's network licence fee.

The ability of NBC, and the other US TV networks, to pay $850,000 in licence fees is likely to continue to decline. The US market for TV programming in 1980 was $2.8 billion (Grieve Horner, n.d.: 109); the UK market in 1982 was £937 million (Broadcasting Research Unit, 1983: 112, 115). And the US market was divided in these proportions: networks 63 percent, syndication 23 percent, PBS 4 percent and Pay TV 9 percent (Grieve Horner, n.d.: 108). But network domination of the US market is under threat. As other terrestrial broadcasters (Rupert Murdoch's Fox/Metromedia is the best but far from the only example) augment their audiences, their share of advertising revenue and their ability to pay for programming at the expense of the networks and pay services (whether delivered by satellite, cable or VCR), the networks' ability to pay high programme-licence fees declines. Grieve Horner project a trend of continuing network decline (see Table 3.7).

As the long period of network oligopoly in the United States draws

Table 3.7 *Share of Viewing Hours by Television Provider*

	1975	1981	1986	1991
Networks	84	75	67	56
Independent and PBS	16	22	22	23
Pay services	—	2	7	13
Non-pay cable services	—	1	3	7

Source: Grieve Horner, n.d.: 4.

to a close, the market structure of the United States will approximate to a model of a plurality of middle-sized distributors each disposing of licence fees for programmes less expensive than those affordable by ABC, CBS and NBC in their heyday. This change in market structure is likely to create increased opportunities for non-US producers to sell into the US market (see the FCC's *New Television Networks: Entry, Jurisdiction, Ownership and Regulation* (1980), which suggests that there are opportunities for a further three profitable television networks in the USA). If the attrition of the networks' share of audiences and revenues continues to be faster than growth in aggregate revenues, then the revenue pool will be shared more evenly among a greater number of players with each player commanding less resources than do the biggest current players. The ability to pay for the production costs of an episode of, say, *Dallas*, at an acquisition cost of $750,000 to $800,000 for an initial screening and $65,000 to $70,000 for a second screening (*Broadcast*, 22 October 1984, p. 70) will decline. But the ability of a greater number of players to pay intermediate prices for programming will rise. In this new regime where very high-cost programming may no longer be afforded and in which demand and ability to pay for low- to mid-cost programming increases, there may well be increased opportunities for sales to the USA by foreign producers. Increases in US distribution capacity (through licensing of new terrestrial broadcasters and satellite and cable-delivered Pay TV) and redistribution of advertising revenue among broadcasters are likely to diminish the comparative advantage of a strong home market resistant to foreign products long enjoyed by US film and TV producers.

There are, of course, counter-indications to this scenario: the merger of a network, ABC, with one of the principal independent groups, Capital Cities Communications (see *Philadelphia Inquirer*, 19 March 1985, p. 1), to form the largest broadcasting group in the US suggests that other resolutions of this contradiction are possible.

Accordingly, the phenomenon of *Kennedy* is likely to become more widely generalized. It was produced by a British company with a British script and made in the United States with United States talent. (*Star Wars* offers a comparable example of a US production in Britain where the US presence was confined to script, director, the four leading players and domicile of the ultimate owner of the production.)

Programme Sales, Regulation and the Levy

It is hard to envisage a role for national regulation in this new order. What role can the IBA (or the Inland Revenue) play with respect to

Grand Central Productions, sales of formats rather than programmes or with respect to a separate company like Zenith, daughter company of Central Television, the holder of the Midlands ITV franchise over which the IBA exercises jurisdiction?

The extraordinary rise in British TV programme sales overseas is indicative of corporate adaptation to a number of factors (see Table 3.8). These include a response to cost inflation and a desire to spread production costs over more than the UK market, as well as a response to the market opportunities offered by the international television programme market and to the Exchequer's levy on ITV non-programme sales profits. It is the latter factor that probably explains the more than proportionate rise in ITCA programme sales *vis-à-vis* those of the BBC. As NERA states of the (pre-February 1986) levy structure and its impact on the ITV companies, 'The optimal tax strategy would be to shift revenues to overseas sales while costs are allocated to national programming' (NERA, 1985).

The levy is the term usually used in the industry to describe the provisions in the Broadcasting Act 1981 (para. 32) for 'additional payments'. The Act provides that annual profits exceeding £650,000, or 2.8 percent of advertising receipts (whichever is the greater), were subject to levy (additional payment) at the rate of 66.7 percent for television contractors. Until February 1986 the levy was not imposed on profits from foreign programme sales, though it is now to apply to such profits at a rate of 22.5 percent and the levy on advertising receipts has been reduced too. The graph in Figure 3.2 illustrates the mismatch between levy and advertising revenues.

In 1982/83 the ITV company with the highest net advertising revenue (Thames Television) was able to escape levy completely. Other members of the ITV 'big five' paid varying amounts of levy, but there is

Table 3.8   *Foreign Programme Sales (£ million)*

| | Year to 31 March | | |
	1979	1982	1984
BBC Enterprises			
Total	7.6	15.7	17.4
USA	1.8	5.6	4.3
Canada	0.6	0.5	0.5
ITCA companies			
Total	29.5	31.5	59.5
N. America	14.4	14.9	42.2

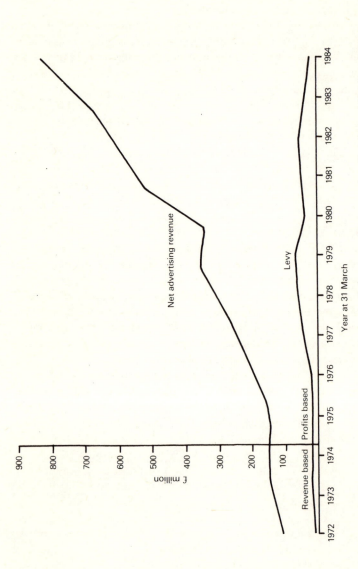

Figure 3.2 *Annual Levy Receipts and Net Advertising Revenue 1972–84 (Comptroller and Auditor General, 1985: 10)*

a clear relationship in the figures between high profits on overseas sales and low levy payments (see Table 3.9).

Table 3.9 *ITV Network Companies, Net Advertising Revenues, Pre-Levy Profits, Profits on Overseas Sales and Levy Payments, 1982/83 (£ thousand)*

Company	Net Ad Revenue	Pre-Levy Profit	Overseas Sale Profits	1982/83 Levy
Thames	115,049	9,032	5,781	0
LWT	79,156	4,758	1,878	10
Granada	93,484	12,409	242	5,377
Yorkshire	71,954	9,260	71	4,387
Central[a]	97,812	4,174	150	211

[a] 1982.

Source: NERA, 1985: 27.

The most striking comparison to be made is that between Thames and Granada. Before levy, Granada's profits — largely from advertising revenue — exceed those of Thames by more than 33 percent. However, Granada loses more than £5 million in levy, Thames nothing. It is unsurprising that between 1982 and 1986 Granada has vigorously pursued a strategy of high-budget production and sales of programmes in foreign markets (e.g. *Brideshead Revisited, The Adventures of Sherlock Holmes* and *The Jewel in the Crown*).

For the future we anticipate that British producers will continue to successfully penetrate foreign television programme markets. It is likely that they will do this in conjunction with foreign co-production partners and that, particularly if successful alliances are concluded with established producers for the US networks, sales to the US networks will become established. The agencies through which these productions are launched are likely to be daughter companies of the ITV franchises and independent producers rather than the ITCA companies themselves in order to escape levy payments. Many of these independent production companies and daughter companies will be located outside the UK as production and consumption of television programmes become more and more international. It makes little sense to ask whether *Kennedy, Star Wars, Finnegan Begin Again* or *Murder in Space* are British (or American or Canadian) productions (or, in another medium, to ask whether *The Economist* is British; or the Frankfurt or New York editions of *The Financial Times* are British). It will make less and less sense to ask that question about more and more television programmes. Culture and cultural production are international phenomena, and the political institutions of the nation-state are highly imperfect tools through which these practices and activities can be controlled and regulated.

The more than proportional rise in ITCA exports of programmes relative to that of the BBC (ITCA rising between 1978 and 1983 from £29.5 million to £59.5 million and BBC Enterprises from £7.6 million in 1978/79 to £17.4 million in 1983/84) suggests that the taxation regime, and in particular the operation of the additional payments' levy bearing on the ITCA companies, has affected their strategy. And the revision of the levy in 1986 was designed both to reduce the tendency to load costs on the domestic side of ITCA companies' activities and take profits from the foreign side and to secure and return to the Exchequer from the companies' foreign sales. It remains to be seen whether the Inland Revenue and the IBA will be able to exact levy either from UK-based companies such as Zenith Films (wholly owned by Central TV but not licensed by the IBA and conducted as an 'at arms length' business with no evident connection to Central's franchise to transmit programmes and sell television advertising time in the English Midlands), to extraterritorial companies such as Thames's joint venture in California, Grand Central Productions, or to sales of intellectual property, such as format rights, which have no direct connection to the franchised activities of an ITV company.

The Importation of Television Programmes by British Broadcasters

The amount of foreign programme material that the BBC may screen is limited by the resolution of the Board of Governors of the BBC (8 January 1981) ensuring that 'proper proportions' of British and foreign programmes are transmitted (*BBC Annual Report and Handbook*, 1987: 239). Neither the IBA nor the BBC are charged with administering a specific quantitative quota by statute.

The IBA requires an 86 percent quota of British and EEC material and permits an additional 1.5 percent of Commonwealth material. It excludes from quota requirements a variety of other categories of programmes, notably films made before 1945 (if shown in a special season), programes dubbed for transmission, sports and news coverage, and programmes deemed to be of outstanding informational, cultural or educational value. The BBC does not state the proportion of its programmes that are of non-British origin, but BBC sources state that the Corporation does not exceed the quota publicly stated by the IBA for commercial broadcasting.

The IBA has supplied weekly averages (hours/minutes) of imported programmes transmitted on ITV and Channel Four by area of origin (see Table 3.10), and state that 'it was estimated that "quota exempt" material in 1984/85 amounted to 11.5% on Channel 4 and 6% on the rest of ITV'. The IBA deem all promotional and advertising material transmitted to be of British origin. Viewing suggests that a small number of advertisements are probably of foreign, mostly US, origin.

Table 3.10   *Weekly Average of Overseas Material (hours and minutes)*

| | Year to 31 March | | | |
	1976	1981	1984	1985
ITV				
Commonwealth	1:17	2:33	2:29	3:20
EEC	0:01	1:10	0:58	0:58
USA/other	11:26	15:13	15:34	14:26
Channel Four				
Commonwealth	—	—	—	0:32
EEC	—	—	1:19	1:37
USA/other	—	—	10:32	9:55

The BBC had not supplied, at the time of writing, comparable figures but, in its analysis of hours of television output for 1984/85 (*BBC Annual Report and Handbook 1986*, p. 147, charts between pp. 150–1), the category, 'British and Foreign Feature Films and Series' accounted for 12.5 percent of output. The categories 'Programmes Produced in London and in the Regions' and 'Open University Programmes' accounted for 79.4 percent and 8.1 percent, respectively. It is clear that the BBC's figures are not readily comparable to those of the IBA but suggest that a large majority of its programming is of UK origin. *British Business* (30 August, 5 September 1985) records the overseas expenditure of the BBC and IBA programme contractors, including Channel Four where appropriate (see Table 3.11).

It can be seen from the table that there was a striking and continuing increase in the cost of programmes acquired from overseas beginning in 1982. Given that the quota administered by the IBA and informally followed by the BBC has remained constant, it seems likely that the increase in transmitted hours following the introduction of TV-am and Channel Four has produced an increased demand for non-British programming. Some of the increase in cost is also undoubtedly due to changes in the dollar–pound parity and the rising cost of programming.

Table 3.11   *Overseas Expenditure by BBC and IBA Programme Contractors
(£ million)*

| | | | Year to 31 March | | | | |
	1979	1980	1981	1982	1983	1984	1985
EEC	6	5	11	9	12	16	13
Other W. European countries	2	4	2	4	4	3	4
N. America	15	18	19	36	47	64	56
Other developed countries	1	1	1	1	1	2	4
Rest of world	4	3	4	5	5	5	5
Total	28	31	37	55	69	90	82

Nonetheless, the rise in expenditure from 1983/84 is remarkable and the reversal of the trend in 1985 is striking.

We have experienced a difficulty in establishing the costs of imported programming similar to that we experienced in establishing the selling prices of British programming. However, some figures are available. *TV World* (1984) gives an average acquisition cost of $7500 to $10,000 per half-hour of programming for the UK and $50,000 to $500,000 as the range of acquisition costs for feature films. Thames Television acquires *Kojak* for a cost of £3000 per programme hour. Channel Four customarily pays between £10,000 and £12,000 for a foreign-language 'art house' feature film (for a two-screening licence). The BBC paid £600,000 for the eight-hour mini-series *The Thorn Birds* and acquires an episode of *Dallas* for $47,500 (*Variety* (23 January 1985) stated that *Dallas* was probably the highest-cost imported programme series screened in the UK). *The Thorn Birds* — or some feature films — cost more than $47,500 per programme hour, but these are very exceptional cases and have production costs higher than even a high-budget, continuing series. The BBC paid £25,000 per hour for the six-hour Canadian mini-series, *Empire Inc*.

British broadcasters pay less than world-market prices for foreign programming because the BBC and ITCA companies (with some rare exceptions) do not bid against each other for the same product. When the BBC and Thames Television engaged in an auction for *Dallas* the cost of *Dallas* escalated to $60,000 per programme hour.

Overall, the positive balance of trade in television programmes between 1979 and 1984 declined. Overseas net earnings by British television companies fell from 1983 to 1984 from £8 million to £1 million. This continued a declining trend from the late 1970s. The decrease in net earnings was largely attributable to an unfavourable balance of trade with North America. It remains to be seen whether the improvement of the balance of trade with North America in 1985 is enduring.

Television Without Frontiers

Broadcasting policy and practice in the UK has characteristically taken place in conditions of national autonomy. To be sure, foreign services (e.g. Radio Normandy and Radio Luxembourg in the 1930s, the pirate radio stations in the 1960s and 1980s) have impinged and provoked adaptation by British broadcasters, but substantially the UK has been able to make its broadcasting history in conditions of its own choosing. That will less and less remain the case. New distribution technologies are creating transnational economic unities in broadcasting to accelerate the transnationalization of broadcasting culture. And transnational political institutions are becoming increasingly important forces — whether for change or for the status quo in the UK broadcasting order. In May 1984 the European Commission adopted a Green Paper, *Television Without Frontiers*, in which the Commission suggests:

(a) that broadcasting is primarily an economic activity which the Commission is therefore competent to regulate under the EEC treaty;

(b) that the Community must ensure that the relevant directly applicable provisions of the EEC treaty (particularly articles 59, 60 and 62) should be respected, so as to suppress all discriminatory and other restrictions on broadcasting from other member states;

(c) that present rules on advertising and copyright are an obstacle to the free flow of television broadcasting between member states; and

(d) that a limited number of measures should be adopted as a first step in the establishment of a legal framework for a single Community-wide broadcasting area in conformity with the treaty's objectives.

The measures proposed by the Commission are:

(a) co-ordination of specific aspects of member states' laws regulating radio and television advertising;

(b) limited co-ordination of member states' copyright laws to ensure that copyright holders' rights to prohibit the simultaneous transmission of programmes coming from other member states are everywhere replaced by rights to receive fair remunerations; and

(c) co-ordination of certain aspects of member states' laws regulating broadcasting in the interests of fair play ('right of reply') and of protecting children and young persons.

The Guardian (10 March 1986) reported the Commission's production of a draft directive which 'aims to sweep away' most national controls and restrictions on broadcasting and stated that the 'guiding hand behind the draft directive belongs to Lord Cockfield the British

Commissioner responsible for opening up the Common Market to genuine free trade'. The proposals for the draft directive, as reported by *The Guardian*, include:

(a) all countries to be obliged to have at least one channel carrying advertising;

(b) no country will be allowed to prohibit television from another, provided it meets certain common standards;

(c) a ban on all tobacco advertising and restrictions on alcohol advertisements;

(d) a common code to protect children by prohibiting all broadcasts that 'involve pornography, gratuitous violence or incitement to race hatred';

(e) a 'made in the EEC' programme quota of 30 percent minimum, rising to 60 percent after three years; and

(f) 5 percent of all programmes to come from independent producers, rising to 10 percent after three years.

There has been, to date, a mixed experience of cross-border television in the European Community. Larger European states, such as France and the UK, have been able to assume that their nationals are consuming almost no television transmitted from outside national territories. West Germany and Italy consume relatively modest amounts of television originated from outside the national territory; West Germany from the German-language services of Switzerland, Austria and the GDR; Italy from Switzerland and the Capo d'Istria services from Yugoslavia. Smaller European countries may consume relatively large quantities of foreign television: Denmark receives broadcasts from Sweden and West Germany; Belgium from France, the Netherlands and West Germany; the Netherlands from Belgium, West Germany and the UK; Ireland from the UK; and Switzerland from neighbouring co-linguists (see Table 3.12).

The proposals of the Commission, if implemented, will require varying degrees of change in the broadcast services of EEC member states. The impact in, for example, Belgium and Denmark, which will be required to introduce television advertising, will be very evident. In spite of the proposals of the draft directive having less impact in the UK, offering UK programme producers considerable economic opportunities and not requiring the statutory 'right of reply' so long opposed by UK broadcasters, the Commission's proposals have found little favour among UK broadcasters. The ITCA's response to the House of Lords Select Committee considering *Television Without Frontiers* is representative:

Table 3.12   *Reception of Foreign Channels (percentages)*

	EEC Estimates	Broadcasters' Estimates
Luxembourg	97	94
Switzerland	n.a.	88
Belgium	84	98
Netherlands	84	82
Denmark	69	63
Ireland	41	44
Italy	35	47
Norway	n.a.	29
Germany	25	34
Greece	16	n.a.
Sweden	n.a.	14
France	14	13
UK	3	neg.

Sources: EEC estimates quoted in *Cable and Satellite News*, January 1984, p. 19; broadcasters' estimates from private communications. Reproduced from Mills (1985).

'The whole tenor of your interesting written submission was, in fact, to me at any rate, that the status quo was working very well and you saw no great reason why it should be altered.'
Mr Plowright: 'Quite right.' (House of Lords, 1985: 207)

It may be that the comments of a number of witnesses to the Lords' Committee to the effect that the Commission's proposals serve principally consumers' interests rather than producers' explain their lack of enthusiasm. The Chair of the Lord's Committee commented that 'the only witness I think we have had before this Committee who comes any way towards praising any element of the Green Paper was the Director of the National Consumer Council' (House of Lords, 1985: 114).

Technological change is rapidly changing the balance of consumption (and the power capable of being exerted by nation-states) of foreign and nationally originated television. *Cable and Satellite Europe* catalogues twenty-seven satellite-delivered services in Western Europe and does not include the Gorizont services originated from the Soviet Union. It is estimated that by 1990 approximately eighty-five low- or medium-power satellite transponders will be available for broadcast service in Europe (Connell, 1985: 216–21), though such estimates should be revised downwards in the light of the grounding of the European launcher *Ariane* and the US space shuttle. Television signals from such satellites require a large receiving antenna for satisfactory reception and it is generally believed that such signals are likely only to be consumed via cable or SMATV systems. However, research performed by Sky Channel and Music Box (reported by Charles Levinson (unpublished) at the 1986 International Institute of Communications Conference) suggests that 97 percent of Dutch cable viewers watch some English-language services (the main ones available are the BBC, Music Box and Sky). In Germany, 91 percent of cable subscribers, in Switzerland 79 percent and Belgium 74 percent consume at least some English-language television.

Of the nineteen channels available on the two principal low-powered European satellites, ECSI and Intelsat 5, a fluctuating number are used as services are launched and closed. Some are scrambled in order to prohibit reception except by a very few subscribers (e.g. the channel distributing live horse racing to UK bookmakers) or to ensure viewers can only obtain the service at economic cost via cable (Sky Channel). Some are financed by advertising (Music Box, Sky Channel, Children's Channel), others are Pay TV (TV5 from France), others are public service operations without advertising (the West German Drei Sat) or with advertising (RAI from Italy). Uptake for these services depends on a variety of factors — cost of reception (whether the signal is scrambled and available on a pay basis), penetration of cable and language of transmission. But it is clear that the UK is both resistant to penetration of foreign services (because of UK linguistic incompetence) and well placed to penetrate other European markets (because of the wide understanding of English). However, the most successful service, Sky Channel, has a deficit of £20 million, and no service approaches profitability yet.

Advertising revenues realized on Sky in 1984/85 were £2.6 million and, for Music Box, £1.5 million; it is estimated that at the beginning of 1986 both Sky and Music Box will be receivable in four million European homes (*The Financial Times*, 14 November 1985, p. 12; 8 February 1986, p. 5). But penetration of services transmitted from low-and medium-power satellites is limited by the extent of cable. Only 8.5 percent of European homes are cabled and only 200 networks have more than 10,000 subscribers. Belgium, the Netherlands and Switzerland are the only highly cabled European countries and account for 66 percent of cabled European households.

To these existing low-power services originated from the UK, Super Channel, programmed by the existing British terrestrial broadcasters, has been added. Equity is provided by the ITCA companies and the BBC is to be paid for the programming it provides and receive a percentage of any profit (though it commits no equity).

High-powered 'direct broadcasting' satellites (DBS) are not yet in operation in Europe, but the West German and French governments both have plans to establish such services soon. DBS requires a much smaller receiving antenna than do existing satellite services and is likely to be consumed by households owning (or renting) their own receivers and by households subscribing to cable services that relay the DBS signals. DBS offers the possibility (as the price of receiving apparatus falls in response to growing volumes of production of receivers) of widespread reception of additional television services in (unlike cable which is and is likely to remain an urban phenomenon) all European locations with access to electricity and a line of sight between satellite and receiving antenna. The French TDFI service was scheduled for launch in November 1986; the West German TV Sat 1 for 1987. German sources estimate that a 120 centimetre dish will be capable of receiving up to forty channels from satellites in the 19° west orbital position. This is likely to be the slot for the 'hot birds' of DBS. The UK orbital slots are in the 31° west position so that UK broadcasters are likely to be disadvantaged.

But optimism about the early establishment of transnational television receivable at low cost has declined. The sole 'heavy' DBS launched by Japan is experiencing problems with its travelling wave tubes (there are it seems unforeseen problems in scaling up these components from the sizes used for low-powered communication satellites), and after the loss of the *Challenger* shuttle and the successive failures of *Ariane* launches no timetable for the establishment of DBS services can be confidently predicted. The shuttle is grounded until 1988 and *Ariane* until 1987. In 1984 insurance for a satellite launch and the first thirty days in orbit cost about 5 percent of insurable value. Now the cost of insurance is 30 percent of value. The French DBS (likely to be the first launched) was scheduled to carry two French-language services and two services provided by Robert Maxwell's European Satellite Television Broadcasting Corporation, one in English, one in Italian. Each channel (to be financed by advertising) is committed to between 70 and 100 hours of original programming per year and is paying £5 million per year per channel for transponders for a contract of eight years duration. Mr Maxwell (the chairman of the company owned equally by Maxwell, Silvio Berlusconi of Italy, Taurus Films of West Germany, TV Cinq the French company headed by Jerome Seydoux of Chargeurs Limitée and by an unnamed Spanish company) stated that

This is the first concrete act by organizations which are not members of the Salvation Army to bring a Europe-wide television programme which will give 123 million European families the opportunity to see European programmes of a kind the Americans have enjoyed for so long. (*The Financial Times*, 13 March 1986, p. 8)

Since Maxwell's licensing for DBS, political control of the government of France has changed and the current French government has attempted to withdraw the licence granted by its predecessor.

In May 1981, the Home Office report, *Direct Broadcasting by Satellite* presented a plan for the use of five channels allocated to the UK in the 11.7–12.5 GHz band at the 1977 World Broadcasting Satellite Administrative Radio Conference. The Home Office recommended that the BBC develop two channels, but that satellite service should be developed 'in a way consistent with our existing broadcasting arrangement'.

Part of the motivation for encouraging an operational DBS system was the desire to stimulate the aerospace and electronics industries and to create a demonstration project that would be useful in selling DBS technology and equipment abroad (see *Hansard*, 20 April 1982). And the Home Secretary commented that any new DBS services would be subject to supervision by a broadcasting authority, and subject to the same programming standards as applied to existing broadcasters (see Cable and Broadcasting Act, 1984, section 42).

Evidence taken at the time of the Home Office report indicated that a consortium of British companies would be prepared to invest private venture capital into the construction and operation of a UK DBS system. However, by 1986, it had become clear that no private interests perceived demand for DBS services to be sufficient to justify investment in a private DBS system.

In February 1986, the Home Office announced that prospective operators of a British DBS system would be free to buy a foreign satellite system. The IBA has advertised the franchise for a service that would provide an initial three channels. The service would be a commercial service dependent on advertising and subscription revenues. The service is not expected to start for three to four years and the prospective franchise operator will need to show that its plan will benefit the UK in economic terms. That is, despite the opportunity to buy a foreign satellite, there must be opportunities for the British space equipment and consumer electronics industries.

British Aerospace is to offer a DBS system for between £100 and £125 million; this is substantially less than the cost quoted in 1985 by Unisat (of which British Aerospace was a member) for a 'gold plated' satellite system, the cost of which inhibited investment in and commitment to a British DBS service (*The Financial Times*, 13 March 1986, p. 8).

Five consortia applied for the British DBS franchise. BSB (Amstrad, Anglia TV, Granada, Pearson and Virgin) planned three advertising-finaced programme packages and a film subscription channel. DBS UK (Carlton, Columbia, Dixons, Hambros Bank, LWT, Robert Fleming and Saatchi and Saatchi) offered three advertising-financed channels to serve groups such as young adults and businesses which were not well served by existing services as well as the Super Channel of UK broadcast repeats. DBL (British and Commonwealth Shipping, Cambridge Electronic Industries, Electronic Rentals, Ferranti, Sears and News International) would transmit a Premium Channel intended for all ages and tastes, a Showcase of home-centred information and entertainment and the existing Sky Channel service. Each channel would be funded by a mix of advertising, pay per view and subscription. NBS (Robert Holmes à Court and James Lee) would offer two advertising-financed channels and a subscription film channel. SAT UK (Bond Corporation, Lonrho, Trillion, Celtic Films) proposed an entertainment channel financed by advertising and a subscription film channel. ITN applied to offer a single-channel news service and Starstream (British Telecom, D.C. Thomson and Thorn EMI) a children's channel (*The Financial Times*, 30 August 1986, p. 3). The contractor licensed by the IBA to provide the UK DBS service is BSB. Other important UK companies are aligning themselves with proposed competitive services (e.g. Thames Television with the Luxembourg service). The transmissions from the UK DBS are to be in C-MAC coding format; those of the French and West German satellites D2-MAC. Reception of French, German and UK services will be conditional on receivers orientated both to the 19° west and 31° west orbital positions and able to decode the C and D2-MAC standards. There will therefore be a tendency for viewers wishing to receive all these services to secure them via cable rather than direct reception. This, however, will not be an option for rural viewers who are likely to remain uncabled.

The difficulties of reception of satellite-transmitted signals should not be underestimated. For example, different orbital positions of satellites require steerable receiving antennae for reception of signals originated from more than one satellite, snow and rain can attenuate signals significantly and larger than 'DBS size' antennae of approximately 91-centimetre diameter are necessary to extend the footprint of DBS services. But it is clear that DBS when established will substantially extend the transnational market for television programming and advertising.

Charles Levinson, now joint Managing Director of Super Channel, stated in evidence to the House of Lords Select Committee on *Television Without Frontiers* that the two UK-originated services transmitted across Europe and North Africa on the ESC1 satellite, Sky and Music Box were 'in Holland . . . in rating terms, equivalent to the national broadcasters or not far below them' (House of Lords, 1985: 172). Similarly Sky Channel claims 10 percent of TV viewers in 'most countries' where it is received (*The Financial Times*, 14 November 1985, p. 12).

The impact of satellite television and transnational advertising on terrestrial services and their income from advertising has been muted by language differences, the scarcity of international brands and the variety of national TV advertising regulations; regulations that have (as a matter of commercial policy) been observed by Sky and Music Box. A representative of the most important transnational television advertising channel — Sky — stated that its advertising came 'roughly one third from American companies, one third Japanese, 20% from mainland Europe and the rest from Britain'. It was claimed that 'nearly all the international names' advertise on Sky, specifically Canon, Digital, NEC, Kodak, Mattel, Nikon, Panasonic, Ford, Toyota, Xerox, Remington, Siemens, Unilever, Colgate and DHL (*The Financial Times*, 14 November 1985, p. 12). But an empirical study of Sky's advertising in 1984 suggests a less impressive achievement. Two of the product categories established by Sepstrup (1985) — 'Chocolate, sweets, gum' and 'Food products' — include 69 percent of the advertised brands and 76 percent of the commercial time sold by Sky Channel. Also 3.1 percent of the advertising time is for *The Sun*, a product of Sky Channel's parent company, News International, which is unlikely to have a wide circulation outside the Anglophone states of Europe (see Tables 3.13 and 3.14).

The European Commission's desire to harmonize and integrate the EEC market for television advertising rests on its view that the Commission has

   (a) a political or moral right to act since broadcasting is relevant to European integration;

   (b) that it has a responsibility under the treaties to intervene in media policy; and

   (c) that it is the EEC which is the proper forum for action and not national or other regional or global groups (House of Lords, 1985: 14).

The Commission's competence in the field of broadcasting is not universally admitted and turns on the provisions of the EEC treaty and

Table 3.13 *Sky Channel: Commercials in February,*
March and April 1984

Brand	Spot Length (secs)	Number of Times Shown	Time of Commercial (secs)	Total Time (secs)	Total Time (%)
Wrigley's PK Gum	30	90	17.8	2700	19.0
Mars Snickers	30	65	12.8	1950	13.7
Sor-Bits Chewing Gum	20	61	12.0	1220	8.6
Bentasil	15	27	5.3	405	2.8
Impulse Perfume Spray	30	25	4.9	750	5.3
Kellogg's Smacks	30	24	4.7	720	5.1
Frolic Dog Food	30	23	4.5	690	4.8
Omega Wristwatch	30	23	4.5	690	4.8
Coca Cola	30	22	4.3	660	4.6
The Sun	20	22	4.5	440	3.1
Freia Milk Chocolate	50	21	4.1	1050	7.4
Freia Rapid Bar	30	19	3.8	570	4.0
Maryland Cookies	30	19	3.7	570	4.0
Wrigley's Juicy Fruit	30	17	3.4	510	3.6
Uncle Ben's Rice	20	13	2.5	260	1.8
Kellogg's Frost Flakes	30	12	2.4	360	2.5
Kellogg's Cornflakes	30	11	2.2	330	2.3
Kellogg's Rice Crispies	30	11	2.2	330	2.3
Scand-Video	30	1	0.2	30	0.2
19 brands	—	506 = 3 hours 59 minutes 45 seconds	100.0	14235	—
Omega identification and clock	10	267 (weeks 5 to 15)	—	—	—

Source: Sky Channel's transmission logs, weeks 5 to 17, 1984, cited in Sepstrup, 1985.

the precedents of the Saatchi and Debauve cases. The House of Lords' Select Committee noted that practically all submissions to it contested the Commission's (and the European Parliament's) competence to exercise jurisdiction over broadcasting.

The Commission (1984: 105) states:

The EEC treaty does not just cover goods but also services. Paragraph 1 of Article 60 of the Treaty defines the concepts of 'services' as follows: 'services

Table 3.14   *Amount and Kind of Advertising on Sky Channel in February, March and April 1984, according to Product Categories*

Category	Number of Brands	% of Brands	Total Time (secs)	% of Time
Books, magazines and newspapers	1	5	440	3
Chocolate, sweets and chewing gum	7	37	8405	58
Soft drinks	1	5	660	5
Food products	6	32	25570	18
Pet food	1	5	690	5
Personal care hygiene	1	5	750	5
Watches, jewellery, glasses	1	5	690	5
Other	1	5	30	0
All products	19	99	14235	99

Source: Sepstrup, 1985.

shall be considered to be services within the meaning of the Treaty where they are normally provided for remuneration in so far as they are not governed by the provisions relating to freedom of movement of goods, capital and persons'.

In the Saatchi case (155/73 1974 ECR), the European Court of Justice held that the transmission of television signals comes within treaty rules on services. In the Debauve case (52/79 1980 ECR), the European Court of Justice found that the treaty's prohibition of restriction on the freedom to provide services within the Community applied to the broadcasting or retransmission of television signals. These rules, though, only prohibit discrimination on the grounds of *nationality*. Thus it is open to the governments of member states to prohibit, for example, advertisements for spirits or programming on grounds of content or quality. The Commission observed (in evidence to the House of Lords Select Committee on the European Communities), 'if some Member States were to prohibit entirely all broadcast advertising whilst others did not, there would be a degree of distortion which is contrary to the whole notion of the Common Market' (House of Lords, 1985: 140). Hence the Commission's desire to harmonize broadcasting regulation across the Community and facilitate transnational flow of programming and advertising.

Critics of the Commission's strategy contest the relevance and appropriateness of its *economic* definition of broadcasting and assert the primacy of broadcasting's cultural and national role. The memorandum to the Lords' Select Committee from the Home Office stressed the difference between broadcasting and 'cross frontier traffic in pig meat or banking' (House of Lords, 1985: Evid. p. 2). Yet the Commission (1984: 6) asserts its competence in cultural questions:

> The EEC Treaty applies not only to economic activities but, as a rule, also to all activities carried out for remuneration, regardless of whether they take place in the economic, social, cultural (including in particular information, creative or artistic activities and entertainment'), sporting or any other sphere.

The Lords' Select Committee recommendations broadly support the retention of national authority over broadcasting and resistance to the initiatives of the Commission for EEC regulation. However, the Lords (1985: 27) also state that 'a system based on individual countries cannot easily co-exist with either of these challenges [i.e. the new distribution technologies and the desire for a European broadcasting market] which are supranational in character'. It is clear that national communication sovereignty is unexercisable in the era of direct broadcast satellites. It is unclear how the UK government will act (whether to support the weight of the Lords' recommendations to resist the Commission's initiatives, to support the Commission or to follow a *laissez-faire* policy). However, if regulation of the new communications order is to be attempted in Europe, it is unlikely to be achieved through bilateral or multilateral agreement between governments and without the Commission and/or European Parliament. Both Commission and Parliament see the policy agenda created by satellite broadcasting as one to be captured for the promotion of European political, cultural and economic integration rather than the defence of existing national prerogatives. The President of the European Parliament, Pieter Dankert, stated in *Televizio* (25–31 October 1982, p. 4) that

> for various reasons, an increasing need for European programmes exists. For European politics it is of enormous importance to be represented by journalists on [the] European level and also to be able to present oneself direct to national audiences. But there are so many more interests — social and cultural — that are from a European standpoint crying out for more intensive and more extensive communication. However, getting this organized is extremely complicated, because Europe has very complicated problems. All sorts of legal problems have to be considered if one seriously looks at the question of the kind of context or structure that would be needed for such a European programme to be able to be implemented, or what kind of framework you would need . . . Europe does not yet exist in the different national consciousnesses.

The main transnational European organizations, the EEC and the Council of Europe, differ in their views of the future of European broadcasting. The Council essentially maintains the rights of nation-states to regulate broadcasting services received within national boundaries. Therefore the laws of the twenty-one member states require to be harmonized so that no existing national provisions are breached. As regards standards of advertising and satellite broadcasting, the Council maintains that advertisers should comply with the law applicable in the country of transmission and, depending on the proportion of the audience which is in another country, should take account of the law of that country. And the Council's recommendations on the principles of copyright law when applied to satellite and cable broadcasting stress conservative considerations:

> States, when they deal with legal issues relating to the transmission of television programmes by satellite and cable, should consider in particular the adverse economic consequences which the use of satellite technology could have on the market for protected works and on the situation of, and employment possibilities for, the right owners involved.

The EEC — notably in *Television Without Frontiers* — argues that national 'rights' (e.g. those of Belgium and Denmark to exclude broadcast advertising) be supplanted by a level European playing-field — a real common market in broadcasting services. The absence of European consensus on a MAC standard suggests that nation-states will continue to negotiate in European fora and act within their own spheres of influence to maximize national advantage rather than create an international European broadcast market. Certainly the UK reception of *Television Without Frontiers* was cool, as has been reaction to the proposal for a European production fund (to produce a Euro *Dallas* among other delights), the establishment of the 'European' right of reply and so on. The ITCA evidence to the Lords' Select Committee argued against such measures, as did the BBC.

There are evident problems in establishing a European consciousness and European programming. Not least is the fact that a number of European states (notably Spain and the UK, though France with the creation of La Francophonie is attempting to consolidate its overseas linguistic community) have cultures that are more closely bound with other non-European countries and cultures than with Europe. The proposals that are integrated in the *Television Without Frontiers* document for the self-conscious programmatic creation of a European consciousness and culture and a freer play of international market forces call into existence an equally grotesque opposing set of Siamese twins: the linking of nationalism and public service. The BBC, for example, in its evidence to the Lords' Select Committee (1985: 68) spoke of: 'the experience of public service broadcasting within Europe and perhaps particularly in the United Kingdom has been beneficial in maintaining and strengthening national culture'.

There is, of course, no more necessity for the coupling of public service broadcasting (the service of a series of minoritarian 'publics') with national culture (the binding together of a majority into a shared 'imagined community' of a national state) than for the linking of a European common broadcasting market with a European culture and consciousness. Rather the shared European consciousness, if one there be, seems most fully realized in the entertainment programming exemplified by *Dallas* which originates from outside the Europe of Community and Council.

CHAPTER FOUR

The Finance of Broadcasting

The Spectrum

> Because radio is a resource which can be shared, because it is a resource which is susceptible to pollution and because it is an increasingly used resource with proliferating applications, some regulatory framework must inevitably be imposed on its use. (Radio Regulatory Division, 1986)

Television is one of the competing uses for the scarce resource — the radio spectrum. This raises the issue of how this resource should be allocated and what charges should be made for usage, since broadcasting is a major consumer of spectrum. For economists this is a standard issue which elicits a standard response — the price mechanism. In the UK this particular solution has been eschewed. Instead 'the general approach adopted . . . has been to issue licences essentially on a first come, first served basis, with a licence fee based on administrative costs' (Radio Regulatory Division, 1986: 6). Here usage is not charged at a rate approximating the value of the spectrum to a user but at what it costs the DTI to run its offices. The Radio Regulatory Divsion's (RRD) (1986: 44) total income in 1985/86 was just over £11.25 million, of which nearly 30 percent came from British Telecom, Mercury, the BBC and the IBA. However, the RRD's costs exceeded its revenue by £5.7 million. The state, then, acts as the allocative mechanism. Its authority is linked to international agreements (due to the 'pollution' problem), and it allows or licenses operators to use a certain proportion of the spectrum for a limited time period and under defined conditions. This authority provides the basis for the government's regulation of broadcasting because it has assumed the property right over the spectrum. Property rights lie at the heart of much economic analysis and are particularly important to the 'liberal' welfare economist like Professor Peacock.

The problems of allocating the scarce spectrum by fiat and at a charge unrelated to the potential economic value to its user are twofold. By ignoring 'opportunity costs' the government is not forcing the user to make the best use of the spectrum. The Peacock report cites an example from the New Zealand Royal Commission on Broadcasting:

'to give away wool for free to those who would use it in the public interest would almost certainly be seen as an inefficient allocation system' (Peacock, 1986a: 31). In effect this method of spectrum allocation is 'crowding out' alternative and potential users. Here lies the second problem because the combination of administrative allocation and non-efficient usage acts as a barrier to entry that is intensified by the growing demand for spectrum space.

It is not surprising that a government committed to high technology and market forces and a parsimonious DTI faced with a deficit from its Radio Regulatory Division should seriously consider some form of pricing mechanism for the radio spectrum. The Merriman review (1984) discussed but rejected the price mechanism. However, a feasibility study on the prospects for market forces as a mechanism for spectrum management is underway. Such a system would replace the judgement of the market for those of bureaucracy and would reflect the values of liberal economists.

The price mechanism would provide some advantages. Firstly, users would be encouraged to 'consume' spectrum space economically, calculating the balance between equipment costs and spectrum charges. There would be an incentive for 'the use of less congested bands . . . which would incur a lower fee' (Barnett, 1986) or even to switch to a completely different form of communication. Some would argue that the price mechanism applied to the radio spectrum would produce the allocative efficiency as is claimed for it elsewhere with use relating to value (see Veljanovski and Bishop, 1983; Adam Smith Institute, 1984).

Currently the British government does make an indirect charge for the spectrum that partially reflects its value to the user. The complex TV levy on the ITV companies claws back some of the earnings derived from spectrum usage. However, the transaction costs of administrating the system are not negligible and, worse, the levy distorts the allocation of costs to programme production by the ITV companies and acts as a disincentive to efficiency. Nor is the levy a stable source of charge incomes, and it represents a declining proportion of ITV income (see National Audit Office, 1985).

An auction for the right to use a segment (or assignment) of the spectrum may improve allocative efficiency and also allow for the abolition of the levy system and its adverse effects. The expected profits from access to the spectrum would be reflected in the price a bidder would be willing to pay. At the same time, the arbitrary nature of the franchises awarded by the IBA to competing companies would be replaced by an auction system. Conceivably, all the public service requirement laid upon the ITV companies by the IBA could still be incorporated in the licence and would be discounted in the price a potential franchisee would be willing to pay. This has also been proposed by the Peacock Committee.

It is clear that as many more uses of the radio spectrum and varying technological means of exploiting it proliferate, spectrum planning without use of the price system becomes increasingly difficult. But the market mechanism is not without its own difficulties. For example, it would be difficult to incorporate public service broadcasting on the BBC model funded by licence fees unless spectrum space was preallocated by the government. The problem for the BBC would be in bidding under a government-determined licence fee, that is, with its total revenue fixed without the ability to charge to viewers (assuming an absence of advertisers). It could not express any derived value to its bid because it would be unable to relate the sum offered to any price payable by viewers.

Additional problems follow from the nature of the competitive process. As we have noted, allocative efficiency requires truly competitive market conditions which in this case mean a large number of alternate and independent potential TV channels competing for the spectrum. As Barnett observes:

> If, however, one assumes that four channels are the limit, and that the current framework is maintained wherever the BBC and the IBA are responsible for administering channels, how might the limited free-market approach work? The options are severely limited by the presence of only two competing organisations, who are hardly likely to attempt to outbid each other to increase their own number of channels at the other's expense. (Barnett, 1986: 9)

Palpably the market conditions of a very large number of potential channels would be a radically different broadcasting environment from that which prevails today.

A major problem with bidding is that the winner, paying the highest price, will expect to extract the highest income by exploiting its position to the maximum. The winner could maximize its revenues, to recoup the bid price, by offering cheap programmes or charging steep fees to advertisers. The latter would ultimately be passed on to the consumer. We should also note that willingness to pay a high price is not necessarily the best credential for operating a TV channel. There are salutary lessons to be learnt from the experiences of the newspaper industry.

Whatever the mechanism of allocating the radio spectrum, its scarcity and the state's assumption of property rights over it provides a rationale for some form of government regulation of broadcasting.

Funding

We need to reiterate two key characteristics of the broadcasting commodity. When a programme is broadcast to the viewer it is broadcast to everyone in the reception area. Viewers cannot be excluded unless special (and expensive) scrambling devices are introduced which, as experience shows, can usually be circumvented. In these circumstances it is very difficult for profit-oriented broadcasters to collect fees or realize profits from viewers *directly*. The second characteristic of the broadcasting commodity is the ever-falling marginal cost within a given reception area of reaching an extra viewer, and the fact that consumption does not cause the product to be destroyed or physically consumed (that is, there are no replacement costs). The standard economic perspective links costs with prices charged. These considerations imply that any fees charged must reflect marginal costs, which are near zero. Not only is it very difficult to collect fees, but the fees themselves on economic criteria are hardly worth collecting. Clearly there is very little incentive for a private concern to enter this market under normal conditions of commodity production so that the broadcasting commodity is not provided. This is termed a 'market failure' — following the public-goods character of the broadcast commodity. Any solution to the funding problem will be 'second best' — a term used by economists to describe the state of affairs where some of the Paretian 'marginal conditions' of optimality are broken[1] and technical inefficiencies arise.

There are three alternative methods of funding broadcasting — some form of taxation (such as a licence), advertising, and Pay TV (whether per channel or per view). All of these are inefficient on strict, Paretian welfare-economic criteria. Each has a particular form of sub optimal outcome consequent of its use. Though it may better reflect consumer choice, Pay TV may be the least efficient since the direct charge produces an immediate divergence from marginal cost. There are other inefficiencies. For instance, Cave concluded that

> the literature on price-excludable public goods shows that unless the supplier is assumed to have perfect knowledge of individual demand curves, the private market charging for the product will undersupply broadcasts, whether that market is organised competitively or monopolistically, and whether or not all units are charged at a uniform price. (Cave, 1985: 26)

Pay TV therefore undersupplies and overcharges.

The licence fee and advertising finance both more nearly meet the zero-charge criterion. It is for this reason that they have been to date the favoured means of funding broadcasting. It is important to stress this point because populist versions of the pro-market argument, widespread in political circles, assume that to be in favour of market disciplines is, at the same time, to favour Pay TV as a means of broadcasting finance.

The Licence Fee

Both the licence fee (or other forms of taxation-based funding) and advertising finance are technically superior to Pay TV as methods of financing broadcasting. The licence fee, however, is not in its turn without its problems. Since TV ownership is a near universal condition, the licence fee is equivalent to a poll tax and has unfortunate regressive elements. This is clear when we compare the proportion of a household's income taken up by the licence fee with that of large international hotels with hundreds of TV sets. This is of course rectifiable. But there are other problems with the licence fee. Because there is no market mechanism for viewers to express choices, it would require a broadcasting authority with omniscience as to audience taste and demand curves to deliver the optimal programming mix. On the realistic assumption that such an authority will not exist, the problems of relating output to consumer demand bulks large and history shows a tendency, especially under monopoly conditions, for elitist tastes to be imposed. Then there is the problem of macro-allocation. How is the optimal level of broadcasting funding to be decided in the absence of any market criteria? The decision is strictly political, not economic, and while there is no necessary economic reason why such a system should undersupply broadcasting — i.e. fail to match potentially expressible consumer demand — there is a tendency for it to do so. This is because of an inertia in a licence-fee system, which sets the fee over a relatively long time period, and then because the elite opinion-formers, who influence such decisions on public expenditure, tend to place broadcasting low on their list of priorities.

There is a distinction to be made between, on the one hand, decisions as to what areas of social expenditure can and cannot reasonably be left to the market and the individual decisions of free economic agents (because of market inefficiencies such as externalities and public goods), and, on the other hand, decisions on the hierarchy of importance imposed on the necessarily social decisions that are unable to be left to the market. For reasons that will become clear, we may want to retain public funding of broadcasting, while at the same time arguing that there is no necessary reason why broadcasting should be seen as less necessary or important than, say, defence or education. A case can be developed here on strong economic grounds for arguing that the licence fee is the best available method of funding and should be expanded because there is an undersupply of broadcasting.

In a recent study, conducted by the IBA using the BARB audience reaction questionnaire, people were asked to attach a monetary value to the programmes they watched. The results are striking. In terms of known TV consumption patterns, the average value attached to a year's viewing was £512. Such results should not be taken too seriously. For one thing, people were not being offered a real concrete choice between two expenditures, and the existence of such potential demand does not mean it will be realized. However, the existence of untapped demand for audio-visual entertainment, provided it is available in a convenient form, can be demonstrated by looking at the effect of the availability of pre-recorded video-cassettes on consumer expenditure on film consumption (see Table 4.1). The £350 million spent on videotaped programmes is a lot more than the income of Channel Four and roughly half the BBC's net licence income for 1984. We should note that broadcast television, cinema attendance and purchase of video-cassettes are not perfectly substitutable activities.

Table 4.1   *Consumption of Feature Films on Video and at Cinemas, 1980 to 1984 (£ million)*

	1980	1984
Sale and rental of videotapes	8	350
Cinema admissions	165	95
Total	173	445

Source: We are grateful to Charles Jonscher of CSP International for this example.

Advertising

In the current UK context many may believe that advertising solves the problem of undersupply better than the licence fee, because in recent years advertising income for ITV has been more buoyant than the politically-determined licence fee. Indeed one powerful element in the debate around the future funding of the BBC has been the assumption that licence-fee revenue cannot keep pace with advertising revenue and hence unless an element of advertising revenue is given to the BBC, its income will become steadily less than ITV's, thus unbalancing the competition between them, upon which, it is argued, the healthy ecology of UK broadcasting rests. This argument has focused on the question of whether the competitive conditions of such a relationship tend to maximize total audiences but restrict óverall programme choice.[2]

Choice and Capacity

Central to the current debate on broadcasting finance and regulation is the claim that the current limitation on competition can only be justified in conditions of channel scarcity stemming from spectrum scarcity. It is then argued that, since DBS and cable are making available limitless channel capacity, a competitive market structure will maximize audience choices and should therefore be introduced.

In assessing this argument we need first to distinguish between the technical availability of channel capacity and the availability of finance to sustain actual broadcasting channels. All the current evidence points to financial constraints as a more powerful limitation on the real availability of broadcasting channels than spectrum availability.[3] This is important because the decision as to which regulatory model optimizes audience choice depends crucially on the number of available channels.

Choice between competing channels is not necessarily the same as diversity of programming because of competitive scheduling. A simple example will serve to illustrate this point. Assume that the audience is split into three types with distinct programme preferences (we could also assume, for simplicity's sake, that they will only watch their first preference). The three types are X with 70 percent potential audience, Y with 20 percent and Z with 10 percent. For broadcasters we assume their aim is to attain the maximum audience size. When there is only one broadcaster it will serve type X and have 70 percent of viewers. When a new broadcaster enters the market it has the choice of taking all of type Y or Z or half of type X. It would choose the latter because the 35 percent audience it would gain is bigger than the 20 percent or 10 percent available in Y and Z. Another entrant would perform the same calculations and again choose market X because a third of 70 percent is bigger than the total of either Y or Z. The effect of increasing the number of suppliers on the types of audience preference served is illustrated in Table 4.2. The minority preference Z does not get served by a new channel until there are at least eight channels under the assumptions posited here, and the eighth entrant may equally choose

Table 4.2   *The Effect of Increasing Channel Capacity on Service to Three Types of Programme Preference*

Number of Channels	Viewer Preference Type					
	X		Y		Z	
	A	B (%)	A	B (%)	A	B (%)
1	1	70.0	—	—	—	—
2	2	35.0	—	—	—	—
3	3	23.3	—	—	—	—
4	3	23.3	1	20	—	—
5	4	17.5	1	20	—	—
6	5	14.0	1	20	—	—
7	6	11.7	1	20	—	—
8	7	10.0	1	20	—	—
or	6	11.7	2	10	—	—
or	6	11.7	1	20	1	10
20	14	5.0	4	5	2	5

A = Channels' serving preference.
B = Percentage of audience for each channel.

to serve type *X* or *Y*. Not until there are twenty channels will there be two meeting the needs of type *Z* preference and then there will be fourteen in type *X* and four in type *Y*.

Much work along these lines has been done in the United States. The number of channels on which, under competitive conditions, alternative minority programmes will be offered, varies according to one's assumptions as to the range and structure of preference and the behaviour of the audience with respect to their second-best choice.[4] We do not deny that a monopoly supplier will not necessarily provide services that match viewers' tastes.

Advertising Finance and Pay TV

The number of available channels not only determines whether competition or monopoly is likely to maximize choice; it also determines the relative desirability of advertising finance and Pay TV.

At first glance Pay TV, assuming its technical feasibility, seems to overcome some of the disadvantages of the other two forms of broadcasting finance. However, the empirical evidence is conflicting. Vogel (1986) provides data on new multichannel cable systems which indicate that some households are willing to pay up to $30 per month for their viewing. But he also cites cases where existing systems have been updated but subscribers have been extremely reluctant to exceed their habitual levels of expenditure on viewing despite increased choice.

It is generally held that Pay TV is likely to produce revenues more nearly matching the total potential revenue available to broadcasting than either licence fees or advertising. For this reason alone, it is attractive to broadcasters. And it is also attractive to welfare economists, especially the liberal variety, because they are uneasy when faced by a market in which individual consumers cannot express the relative weight of their demands through a price mechanism. Pay TV does not, however, escape from the zero-cost public-good argument.

Studies comparing advertising-financed channels with pay channels show that pay achieves greater programme variety at the expenses of suboptimal consumption levels (see Burns and Walsh, 1981). This means that the price charged naturally excludes viewers to a level below that justified by the relevant direct costs of programmes. Advertising-supported channels and Pay TV systems both exhibit a bias against high-cost programmes and small groups of highly appreciative viewers.

In the end what the result of such studies come down to is that the higher the number of available channels the greater the advantages of pay and of competition, the lower the number of channels the greater the advantages of advertising and monopoly.[5] This is why the existence or otherwise of spectrum scarcity is so crucial to arguments about the relative desirability of differing economic structures (monopoly, duopoly or competitive) for broadcasting, and why it is necessary to stress that it is not just spectrum scarcity that determines the number of broadcasting channels that can in reality, as opposed to in a model, be made available.

Though it can be argued that Pay TV provides wider choice, there are two caveats. Firstly, choice is achieved at some cost. Choice through exclusion, providing the means for the TV operator to collect fees, requires a device for exclusion. Scrambled signals must be encoded and decoded which necessitates more capital equipment in the system, and the resources used here could be used elsewhere, even in broadcasting, so there is a welfare cost. The Peacock Committee, in studying exclusion devices in the United States for Subscription TV (STV), observed that 'the scrambling technologies used are also fairly primitive. Typically, they are some version of the "sync suppression" kind, costing approximately $120 per household and by no means cheat proof' (Peacock, 1986a: 111). To these must be added the transaction costs of collecting fees, disconnecting non-payers, customer service, billing, telephone enquiries etc. Again using the United States as an example, the Peacock Committee cited the following: 'According to one US estimate, such costs amount to $33 per subscriber (in 1982 prices) for a STV system with 50,000 subscribers — about 12 percent of revenue' (Peacock, 1986a: 112). The second caveat concerns the nature of choice. Obviously more channels will provide more choice between channels but not necessarily between programmes. Whereas monopolies and duopolies can pursue complementary scheduling strategies, Pay TV channels may provide very similar fare. The attractiveness of Pay TV therefore depends on the quality of choice and the costs of achieving choice.

It may be that regulated and uncompetitive systems, or even monopolies, deliver more variety in programming. A study commissioned by the Peacock Committee (1986a: 74–80) concluded that 'the range of programming available to all the population in the UK ... is among the most extensive provided by the major broadcasting systems throughout the world' (Peacock, 1986a: 75).

However, there is no guarantee that this potentiality will be realized in a regulated or monopolistic system or that the range of programming offered will correspond optimally to the range of programming demanded by audiences. A dominant characteristic of the broadcast market (whether its allocations are performed by competition among suppliers or regulation) is the imperfect signalling system from consumers to suppliers. There is, in regulated public service systems, a potential for elites to 'capture' the system and offer a range of programming — which may be highly varied — which corresponds imperfectly to the range desired by audiences. The historical experience of public service broadcasters in Europe has characteristically been that of experiencing a loss of audiences to new competition, readjusting their programme schedules and rebuilding audiences around a different range of programmes. A good example is the BBC's response to the American Forces Network in World War II, to the radio pirates in the 1960s and pre-eminently to ITV in the mid-1950s. The experience of RAI in Italy and TROS, followed by the other major Dutch broadcasting societies in a rush of 'Trossification' (Ang, 1985) were similar.

The national newspaper industry in the UK is experiencing a period of 'hot' competition and is distinguished by a number of new titles — nationally *Today* and *The Independent* and in London the *Daily News,*

Sunday Sport and the revived *Evening News*. Of these though *Today, The Independent* and *Sunday Sport* are the only titles to emanate from formations of capital new to the newspaper industry, and *Today* has come under the influence of Lonhro (which owns *The Observer*) and, most recently, Rupert Murdoch's News International. But the change in the cost structure of the industry has permitted the entry of new corporations and new voices; for how long is a moot question.

In the broadcasting sector, long-term outcomes are similarly uncertain. The development of relatively low-cost satellite distribution of television signals permits economies of scale in distribution to be realized over larger geographical areas. The public-good characteristics of British broadcasting no longer end at Dover but are actually and increasingly realized over continental Europe. Of course, there are formidable cultural and linguistic barriers to a wide consumption of signals in countries other than those of the signals' origin. But the effect of a greater plurality of signals is to reduce audiences for any given signal to reduce revenues at the same rate for any given signal in any national market. Either this reduction in revenues occurs directly in an advertising-financed system or indirectly in increased political resistance to raising licence fees to fund services that are less and less watched. Advertising-financed signals can (assuming that the political process of creating a European advertising market for broadcasting is successfully completed) sell transnational audiences to advertisers and, potentially at least, experience no diminution in revenue. But this process is easier said than done (not least because of the paucity of transnational brands), and the short-term effect of transnational provision of television signals is to threaten the revenue base of existing broadcasters while offering no secure funding for the new services. It seems likely therefore that both existing and new services are likely to experience pressure on revenues and costs and to reduce expenditure on programming. A long-term effect may be the division of a fixed or slowly growing sum of revenues over a greatly increased number of channels with a consequent fall in the revenues per hour of programming. A fall in revenues necessarily requires a reduction in costs and a likely increase in the number of repeats screened, archives recycled and programmes purchased on the international market which originate from less competitive markets where production costs have been recouped and the products are available for acquisition at close to marginal cost.

The national press is highly concentrated (a horizontal oligopoly) with a small number of groupings effectively controlling the market. In the provincial press where the new technology is frequently used, and which forms the technological basis of Jay's thesis (see Peacock, 1986a: 112–18), concentration is also very high. In 1984 the five largest groups were responsible for 60 percent of the total circulation of the seventy-eight paid-for evening titles, and half the sales of the paid-for English and Welsh provincial morning papers (Goodhart and Wintour, 1986). The national control is facilitated by a hold over the distribution channels. Since it is essential for profitability to control access to audiences via distribution, such channels of distribution are mono-polized. Thus the so-called free press sector — which Peter Jay in evidence to the Peacock inquiry would like to take as a model for broadcasting — is characterized by the oligopolistic control of a few major media corporations, such as News Corporation. Current technical changes, by reducing production costs and thus lowering barriers to entry and the circulation level at which newspapers move into profit, are likely to produce, as one would expect, a restructuring of the market. Unless firm government action is taken, the same oligopolistic tendencies are likely to reassert themselves.

We know that the UK supports a higher proportion of programming than any other country apart from the US, and possibly Japan. We also know that the number of channels and the proportion of programming is closely related to the size of the domestic market. Thus, while satellite technology, whether DBS or linked to cable distribution systems, may raise the number of channels supplied to a given country, this can only be done if the programmes are repeats, or imported at a lower cost than existing domestic production and/or the investment in existing original production is lowered. While choice may appear to rise within a distinct national market, it may, at the same time, be lowered in the international market. It is no accident that the two most highly cabled countries in Europe, Holland and Belgium, are both small countries that cannot sustain a wide range of domestically produced choice and thus find advantages in importing programming from neighbouring countries at low to zero marginal cost. If we look at the international film market we will see an industry operating under largely unregulated, free market conditions, in which the US justice department has forcibly separated the major distribution and exhibition divisions. And yet over the years since this break-up, the number of films distributed on the world market by the US majors has declined, while their market share has grown to include a dominant position not only in the cinema, but also in the supply of programmes to the TV, cable and video-cassette markets.

It may be argued that none of this matters, or that it is inevitable. Indeed, it can be cogently argued that UK broadcasting is living above its station. It is far from clear that diversity, widening of choice and responsiveness to audience demand are the only outcomes of a more competitive broadcasting environment, whether competition is delivered on a pay-per-view (or channel) or advertising-financed basis.

The microeconomics of cultural production tend to develop towards oligopolistic structures even with new electronic technologies. In the absence of an active competition and takeover policy, small groups will still dominate cultural commodity production just as in many other industries, but the product will not become just like any private good. Technology may provide an escape from spectrum scarcity, but economic forces will ensure that the ownership and control of channels will be concentrated in a relatively small number of enterprises.

Notes

1. See Nath (1973) for a brief introduction to the second-best issue.
2. Several models are tested and under various assumptions support this position in Owen et al. (1974).
3. See, for example, IBA (1985) and ITCA (1985). There is, of course, a 'he would say that, wouldn't he' element in this evidence. However, independent reports also supported the view that the advertising case would shrink if the BBC carried advertising (see, for example, NERA, 1985).
4. See Cave (1985), for a valuable résumé of this work. See also Owen et al. (1974).
5. This conclusion follows the analysis of Steiner (1961), but the assumptions about viewing patterns are important to the results.

CHAPTER FIVE

The Peacock Report

The *Report of the Committee on Financing the BBC* (Peacock, 1986a) maintains a long and honourable tradition in British government commissions and committees of inquiry in exceeding its brief. The Peacock Committee delivered a comprehensive and radical assessment of the structure and regulation of the whole British broadcasting order.

Peacock received a very bad press in Britain. The opposition spokesman on broadcasting, Gerald Kaufman, described it as 'a jumble of evasive verbiage'. He said 'the proper place for this report is not the pigeonhole but the wastepaper basket' (*The Financial Times*, 4 July 1986), and a government minister was quoted as saying 'we're going to kick it into the long grass' (*The Financial Times*, 5 July 1986). The report has pleased few interests. The right is disappointed by the report's arguments that the BBC must remain large so as to resist government pressure, that broadcasting requires no moral censorship other than that prescribed by common and statute law, and that advertising finance for the BBC is neither likely to lead to a system that more perfectly achieves consumer satisfaction nor is the advertising 'cake' in the UK sufficiently large to fund the BBC without adverse effects on other media. The left is displeased by the Peacock report's advocacy of the market and consumer sovereignty, and its assault on public sector institutions.

It is not our intention to join the chorus of voices attacking Peacock. The report is the most intellectually considerable attempt to grapple with broadcasting policy published by the UK government for many years. It can be compared to the Pilkington report of 1962 which made as intellectually serious a case for an administered public-service vocation for broadcasting as does the Peacock report for a new market regime.

There are absurdities in Peacock; notably its advocacy of a £10 to £15 billion investment in a broadband cable infrastructure in order to achieve a more perfectly competitive market than now exists. Here the cure may be worse than the disease. Already some backtracking is under way; Alan Peacock (1986b) suggests that a 'table-d'hôte' programming regime (that is, a schedule of programmes constructed by broadcasters and with little or no possibility of audiences exercising choice) may offer better value than an 'à la carte' system (that is, a regime in which audiences can construct their own schedule of programmes to their preferred mix from a wide range of choices), implicitly recognizing that the costs of establishing a competitive system may not be worth paying. It is the radicalism of the Peacock report that has attracted the contumely of commentators. Peacock is the first government report to critically examine what it calls the 'comfortable duopoly' (para. 197) of British broadcasting and to urge a broadcasting order dedicated: 'to enlarge both the freedom of choice of the consumer and the opportunities available to programme makers to offer alternative wares to the public' (para. 547).

Clearly, and as the authors of the report recognize, these are political questions as much as they are economic ones. And there is in Peacock, properly, a political motivation and a political economic concern that extends beyond broadcasting. A prominent, and controversial motif of the report was its attack on the status quo as a 'comfortable duopoly'. Samuel Brittan, a leading member of the committee, brother of the Home Secretary who appointed the Peacock Committee and principal economic commentator and assistant editor of *The Financial Times* elsewhere has characterized the UK economy (and society) as: 'a dual economy of insiders with well paid secure jobs and outsiders who drift between ill paid labour and the dole' (*The Financial Times*, 20 November 1986). Although the gap between the haves and have-nots in British broadcasting is smaller than that between the extremes of wealth and poverty in British society, Brittan's image corresponds to the way in which some independent producers — the 'outsiders' — experience their relation to the BBC and ITCA companies — the 'insiders'.

Peacock's attack on the status quo has often been perceived as an attack on public service broadcasting. The committee stressed that such was not its intention for its project of enlarging consumer choice and opportunities for new voices and new products to enter the broadcasting market-place depends on public service broadcasting: 'The fulfilment of this goal so far from being incompatible with public service activities positively requires them in a sense of public service' (para. 547).

The committee is not necessarily to be taken at its word, and its version of public service broadcasting demands critical interrogation, not least because its proposed public service broadcasting council (PSBC), which is intended to provide programmes and services squeezed out by the operation of a market regime when 'well before the end of the century subscription should replace the licence fee' (para. 673), appears little different to the often criticized Arts Council of Great Britain. But whether or not the claims of Peacock can be finally sustained, it is abundantly clear that its conception of the nature of public service broadcasting, of the proper relation of consumers (viewers and listeners) to producers (broadcasters and programme makers) and of the long-sanctified institutions of British broadcasting is very different to that of its predecessors. Indeed Peacock regards the existing order as a system of self-perpetuating privilege exercised by insiders in their own rather than the public interest. Here too the committee's analysis corresponds to the wider political-economic analysis advanced by one of its most prominent and vigorous members, Samuel Brittan, who refers to a global 'corrupting effect of interest group pressures on the moral legitimacy, practical effectiveness and, ultimately, the very stability and sustainability of liberal democracy' (*The Financial Times*, 20 November 1986). But the requirement that there be 'regular and frequent turnover in the membership of the Council' (that is, the PSBC) offers scant protection against interest group pressures.

The Annan Report

Before discussing Peacock's analysis of and recommendations for British broadcasting, we turn to consideration of the rationale of the public service system that forms that status quo. Before Peacock the most recent substantial inquiry into broadcasting was that chaired by Lord Annan; the Committee on the Future of Broadcasting was appointed in 1974 and reported in 1977. The Annan Committee represented itself as a pragmatic body and justified its recommendations on the grounds of practical politics rather than abstract principle. Accordingly, what was stressed in the report was the maintenance of the then-existing broadcasting order and modest adaptation within it. Annan (1977) stated that the first of its objectives was 'to preserve British broadcasting as a public service accountable to the public through Parliament. This tradition has long been accepted by the nation and our recommendations are to strengthen it' (para. 30. 1). Annan received the reception it sought; the Home Secretary greeted it thus: 'what impressed me most about the report . . . is what the committee did not recommend. It did not recommend any fundamental changes in the institutional arrangements for broadcasting in this country.'

Though Annan stated that it sought to devise a structure within which broadcasting in the UK could develop, it neglected to consider new distribution technologies and offered as its innovations the introduction of new 'authorities' within the existing broadcasting order so as to realize a philosophy of pluralism. Indeed the Annan report was a conservative document articulating no new principles for broadcasting.

We must return to the early 1960s — as the Peacock Committee did (para. 30) — for a vigorous and clear statement about the philosophy of UK broadcasting before Peacock and about the intellectual and organizational foundations of UK broadcasting.

The Pilkington Report

The Pilkington Committee on broadcasting was appointed in 1960 and reported in 1962. Its conception of the role and function of broadcasting has dominated broadcasting policy in the UK up to Peacock. Pilkington conceived of the audience for broadcasting services as a collection of victims needing protection from television (and the committee chose to regard television as paradigmatic of broadcasting). Television was judged to be a 'main factor in influencing the values and moral standards of our society' (para. 42) and audiences were characterized as distinguished by their vulnerability. Pilkington cites a submission by the Workers' Educational Association (WEA) which asserts that 'going to a cinema or a theatre, buying or borrowing a book or a magazine involves a conscious critical approach'. But Pilkington observes that 'the television audience is vulnerable to influence in a way that readers of newspapers and cinema audiences are not', and glosses the WEA contention by stating that 'sitting at home, people are relaxed, less consciously critical and therefore more exposed' (para. 41). Accordingly, the need to protect vulnerable audiences is taken by Pilkington as a major support for its rationale of 'authority' as a principle of regulation. Its conception of the audience as vulnerable and requiring protection is antithetical to Peacock's robust championship of the sovereign consumer. There is a fundamental difference in conception of the 'polis', of the role and power of the individual, between Pilkington and Peacock. The different political judgements that identify the television viewer variously as passive and vulnerable or active and robust do not readily correspond with British party political alignments. Rather than being susceptible to comfortable appropriation by either of the dominant UK political parties,

Peacock signals the end of the long intellectual and political consensus in the UK on the role and organization of broadcasting and sets uncomfortable questions for all those, whether broadcasters or politicians, with a stake in the status quo.

The second leg of Pilkington's rationale for 'authority' is its conception of the audience for broadcasting as a differentiated collection of 'publics' (Reith's term), not a unitary public. The committee's analysis and programme is the most trenchant and persuasive instance in an extensive lexicon of advocacy for public service broadcasting:

> 'To give the public what it wants' seems at first sight unexceptionable. But when applied to broadcasting it is difficult to analyze. The public is not an amorphous, uniform mass; however much it is counted and classified under this or that heading, it is composed of individual people; and 'what the public wants' is what individual people want. They share some of their wants and interests with all or most of their fellows; and it is necessary that a service of broadcasting should cater for these wants and interests. There is in short a considerable place for items which all or most enjoy. To say, however, that the only way of giving people what they want is to give them these items is to imply that all individuals are alike. But no two are. Each is composed of a different pattern of tastes, abilities and possibilities; and even within each person the emphasis on this or that part of the pattern is not always the same. Some of our tastes and needs we share with virtually everybody; but most — and they are often those which engage us most intensely — we share with different minorities. A service which caters only for majorities can never satisfy all, or even most, of the needs of any individual. It cannot, therefore, satisfy all the needs of the public. (para. 44)

Pilkington's conception of the audience is of a differentiated plurality of groups, membership of which is constantly in flux. The proper role of broadcasting services is therefore to maintain this minoritarian pluralism by offering a varied programming mix. The variety in programming will in turn enable individuals in the audience to migrate to new groups of viewers or listeners and thus to form new 'publics' and fulfil the need for broadcasting to offer its consumers a chance to develop (and improve) their tastes. The ascent of the cultural pyramid (see Haley, 1948) by the British has, in Pilkington's judgement, been led by broadcasting:

> We have seen in the past thirty years the development of a widespread interest in symphony concerts which could never have been predicted; competitive swimming both as a pursuit and as a spectacle has captured the public's interest in an even shorter time; where interest in classical literature was all but dead, now there has been a sudden demand for pocket translations of the classics. In each instance to have denied the public the

chance to develop the taste would have deprived many of pleasures — in short would have deprived them of 'what they want'. (para. 47)

The proper role of broadcasters then is not to respond to the current desires of audiences but to lead them to new experiences and enable them not simply to like what they get but, on the basis of wider and deeper knowledge, to get what they like. To give 'the public what it wants' is 'patronising and arrogant' (para. 48); rather it is the broadcasters' duty to 'respect the public's right to choose from the widest possible range of subject matter and so to enlarge worthwhile experience' (para. 49).

The question that follows these precepts is 'how?' What institutions best realize these ends? Pilkington believed (though it identified some areas where competition had been beneficial) that competition did not maximize welfare in broadcasting: 'the pressure of competition has sometimes caused the Corporation, consciously or unconsciously, to depart in practice from its own ideal of public service broadcasting' (para. 147). And Pilkington noted that commercial television: 'falls well short of what a good public service of broadcasting should be' (p. 67). Here Pilkington accepts the worth of the broadcasting institutions in place in the 1960s, though with some criticism, particularly of the ITA (which later became the IBA). The BBC and ITA are 'to act as Trustee for the national interest in Broadcasting' (para. 402) and exercise their trusteeship through the authority of their governing boards to whom the broadcasting corporations are answerable. It is the boards (the governors of the BBC and the members of the ITA) which are the end point of the chains of power and action articulated in Pilkington. Indeed Pilkington recommended extension of the ITA's powers in order to redress the deficiencies it perceived in ITV. Pilkington discusses at length the role of the boards and the qualities required in their members (without considering either that appointment is owed by governors and members to the Prime Minister's patronage or the overrepresentation on the boards of wealthy, public-school educated ex-officers and Oxbridge graduates. Pilkington states that

> the Governors' and Members' concern is to represent and secure the public interest in broadcasting. It is for them to judge what the public interest is, and it is for this that they are answerable. They must not do so by assessing the balance of opinion on this or that element of programme content, and then adopting the majority view as their own; for as we have already noted, this would be to mistake 'what the public wants' in the misleading sense implied when the phrase is used as a slogan — for the public interest. Their task is, as we have said, to be thoroughly aware of public opinion in all its

variety, to care about it and to take proper and full account of it. Having done so, they must then identify the public interest in broadcasting, defined as the fullest possible realisation of the purposes of broadcasting, and secure it through control of the executive arm. (para. 408)

It is clear that governors (and members) are to act as Platonic guardians, resisting the siren call of the 'majority view' and resolutely discharging their lonely duty of defining and securing the public interest. The costume of guardian is not one we simply conjure into existence for polemical purposes by adroit selective quotation from a report of a quarter of a century ago, but is the working habit of senior broadcasters. The Chairman of the IBA when innocently asked in 1982 by an eminent Canadian communication scholar 'How do you decide what is the public interest?' replied 'I have been appointed to this office because I know what the public interest is'. Recent broadcasting history is replete with examples (some noted by Peacock) that echo these sentiments.

The Peacock Report

The Peacock report challenges these long-dominant assumptions. Its analysis and organizational programme proceeds not from the Siamese twins of a passive and vulnerable audience and a guardian authority, but from the point of view of a sturdy and independent consumer/ viewer. It sees the public interest as best defined by the public itself and the role of administration and politics as the creation of an arena in which consumer sovereignty may best be defined and practised. It believes that the public service vocation of broadcasting will be best realized by competition between rival suppliers, and that the offer of new perspectives and experiences to 'publics' through innovatory programming (which was regarded by Pilkington as a justification for broadcasting by 'authority' because it was unlikely to be supplied in a market regime devoted to giving audiences what they want) is likely to best be achieved through competition which 'provides further benefits to the public through the incentive given to new and improved services' (para. 123).

This radical departure from the old order has afforded Peacock a good deal of opprobrium. But a substantial new agenda for the discussion of broadcasting policy in the UK has been put in place by the Peacock report. It is to an assessment of the quality of recommendations and argument of the Peacock report that we now turn.

The Peacock Committee's discussion of the funding of the BBC by advertising is generally regarded as a strong element in its report. No serious challenge either to the terms of the discussion or to its conclusions has been mounted. The committee noted that the UK is among a cluster of countries in which expenditure on television advertisements accounted for a high proportion of total advertising expenditure (UK 31 percent, Australia 33.7, Italy 36.9, USA 32.9), and that in other European countries TV advertising spending was a significantly lower percentage of total spending on advertising. The report further observes that while there has been a close relationship between advertising expenditure and GNP in the UK, advertising expenditure has grown more rapidly than GNP. In a survey of a variety of studies of the UK advertising market, the Peacock Committee agreed with the conclusions of two separate studies (NERA, 1985; Cave and Swann, 1985) which indicated that the short-term effect of an increase in the supply of slots for broadcast advertising would be a reduction in total broadcast-advertising revenue. Overall the committee judged that the effect of TV advertising on the BBC would be to make it 'more difficult than otherwise for newspapers to attract advertising. In the longer run more competition in the advertising market will put pressure on all branches of the media either to reduce costs or to reduce their scale of operations' (Peacock, 1986a: para. 418). In particular pressure would be experienced by the smaller ITCA companies, Channel Four and S4C, and no necessary increase in allocative efficiency would be realized:

> An advertising supported system will lead to programme diversity only to the extent that different advertisers are willing to pay to associate their messages with different programmes. The important point from an efficiency perspective is that there is no reason why the value of programmes to advertisers should correspond to the value attached to programmes by viewers and listeners. (Peacock, 1986a: para. 421)

Peacock's argument against advertising as a means of funding the BBC is twofold. Pragmatically the committee recognize that advertising on BBC will not generate sufficient revenue to fund the BBC without seriously damaging the finances of the other UK media. But more fundamentally advertising finance means that the interests of advertisers rather than viewers and listeners will tend to be prioritized.

Accordingly, the committee recommended (Recommendation 2) that 'BBC television should not be obliged to finance its operations by advertising while the present organization and regulation of broadcasting remain in being'. But that (Recommendation 7) 'the BBC should have the option to privatise Radios 1, 2 and local radio in whole or in part. IBA regulation of radio should be replaced by a looser regime.' The majority of the committee recommended that 'Radio 1 and Radio 2 should be privatised and financed by advertising.' This recommendation is strangely at odds with the committee's critique of advertising finance and hard to realize since it is unclear what would be sold in the privatization process: the main assets of Radio 1 and 2 — the frequencies on which services are broadcast — do not belong to the BBC.

Peacock recommended a series of changes to the licence-fee funding of the BBC. Most important was the suggestion that the licence fee should be linked to the retail price index. The committee stated that it wished to achieve both an insulation of the BBC from governmental pressure (setting the level of the licence fee is a powerful instrument of control in government's hand) and provide incentives for the BBC to contain its costs and maximize its revenues. The Peacock proposal makes sense in both respects (though there is no clear relation between the movement of retail prices and broadcasting costs, the RPI seems no less imperfect a yardstick to use in respect of broadcasting than it is in telecommunications where British Telecom's basket of tariffs is permitted to rise by the RPI minus 3 percent). It was recommended (Recommendation 4) that the BBC appoint the collection and enforcement agent for the licence fee. Again this is a sensible, pragmatic proposal — in 1984/85 the Post Office charged 5.5 percent of licence-fee revenue for its collection and enforcement services. It seems likely that the BBC could get a better deal in a competitive regime. Recommendation 5, that a licence fee be levied on car radios, is an ambiguous recommendation, but a member of the Peacock Committee has explained that the committee intended a once-and-for-all payment levied on new cars and not an annual payment required from all car radio users. The committee also suggested (Recommendation 6) that all pensioners drawing supplementary pensions in households wholly dependent on a pension should be licence-fee exempt. The last two recommendations, though undoubtedly of importance to those who win and lose them, are unlikely to make a significant impact on the finances of the BBC.

In respect of commercial television, Peacock recommended (Recommendation 10) that franchises for ITV contracts be issued after competitive tendering. As the committee stated, 'this last recommendation is an important one'. The competition for tenders would have the merit of raising the revenue accruing to the consolidated fund from broadcasting. The ITV contractors have demonstrated an impressive ability to structure their businesses so as to minimize their liability to tax and levy. Peacock's proposal would cheaply and unavoidably secure a return to the public for the use of its property — the radio spectrum — enjoyed by commercial television contractors. Peacock made it clear that the IBA should establish minimum performance standards for TV contractors and that franchises remain subject to regulation by the IBA. However, three committee members dissented from this recommendation, pointing out cogently that in the event of a franchisee going out of profit its performance undertakings to the IBA would be unsustainable and unenforceable and, as we state elsewhere in this study, ability to pay for a TV station is no indication of merit or competence to run one.

Such franchises were to be awarded (Recommendation 11) on a rolling-review basis with the effect that franchisees performing to the IBA's satisfaction would enjoy their franchise for the whole of its duration, but that unsatisfactory performers might, after due notice, experience premature termination. Also (Recommendation 12) franchises were awarded for ten years. These two recommendations seem modest and unexceptional. They give the IBA more effective regulatory power than it currently enjoys. But the regulator will still be faced — should it wish to terminate a franchise for imperfect performance — with the necessity of finding a replacement contractor if an ITV area is not to be deprived of a channel of television and of admitting its own initial mistake in franchise allocation. None of these proposals address the existing imbalance of funding between the BBC and commercial television. Competition between the BBC and ITV is not competition on equal terms, and the effect on the BBC's labour costs exerted by commercial television (which can afford to pay more and therefore drives up prices which the BBC is compelled to follow) was not considered by the committee.

Peacock made two (or perhaps three if Recommendation 17 is included) 'deregulatory proposals' — Recommendation 16 that non-EEC nationals be permitted to assume cable franchises and Recommendation 18 that the general provisions of common and statute law relating to obscenity, defamation etc. apply to broadcasting rather than the specific provisions of the broadcasting acts prescribing the IBA's right and duty to pre-vet programmes. Both these proposals are controversial; the 1986 Labour Party Conference resolved that foreign nationals should not be permitted to own a controlling interest in any British TV, radio, satellite, cable or newspaper company. And influential sections of the Conservative Party have attempted to extend the moral regulation of broadcasting.

Peacock's remaining recommendations are all directed towards intensifying competition in UK broadcasting. The BBC and commercial broadcasting should (Recommendation 9) cede their unused spectrum rights — between 1.0 a.m. and 6.0 a.m. — to other users and new users pay for their use of spectrum space. This measure, if implemented, offers a low-cost entry to the broadcasting market for new services and introduces explicitly (as does Recommendation 10 for the auction of ITV franchises) the principle of charging for spectrum use with proceeds accruing to the Treasury. Recommendations 7 and 7a extend this principle reducing the regulation of independent local radio (ILR) by the IBA and permitting the BBC to privatize local radio and Radio 1 and 2. But radio falls outside this study's remit and we do not comment on Peacock's proposals for radio.

Recommendation 8 proposes that over a ten-year period the BBC and ITV procure at least 40 percent of programming from independent UK producers. If implemented successfully it is likely that the programme market would become more competitive and that new entrants would find it easier to sell programmes and establish businesses. Also it is possible that diversity of programming would be enhanced and that pressures for cost reduction would be exerted on BBC and ITV production. However, 40 percent is an enormous proportion; if we assume that 84.5 percent of programme output is of UK origin (strictly of EEC origin), Peacock is proposing that almost half be produced out of house whereas now most BBC and ITV programming is produced in house (in 1982 BBC1 screened 17 percent and BBC2 22 percent of out-of-house productions (BRU, 1983: 115)). In 1985/86 ITV screened 11 percent UK out-of-house productions and Channel Four 41.25 percent UK out-of-house productions (*IBA Annual Report and Accounts 1985/86*, p. 32). The independent producers' pressure group established after Peacock reported campaigns for only 25 percent of BBC and ITV UK programming to originate from independents.

Recommendation 14 proposes that Channel Four should be able to sell its own advertising and cease to be funded by the ITV contractors. This recommendation is designed to make Channel Four independent of the ITCA companies. It currently enjoys a protected status, its income determined by the IBA and levied from the ITCA companies; it may be that Channel Four will prefer retention of its current status to an uncertain reliance on directly selling audiences to advertisers. And the changed regime is one in which Channel Four would be more dependent than it now is on satisfying advertisers and no more responsive (perhaps less) than it is now to the desires of viewers.

The remaining recommendations (1, 13, 15, 17) are to promote an increased penetration of new distribution systems and thus ensure the exposure of the terrestrial broadcasters to increased competition. Recommendation 1 requires installation of a peritelevision socket in all new TV receivers so as to ease attachment and lower the costs of descramblers should Subscription TV (whether pay-per-view or per-channel) be introduced. Recommendation 13 requires that DBS franchises be allocated by tender. Arguments similar to those (Recommendation 10) for the allocation by tender of frequencies for commercial terrestrial broadcasting are advanced by Peacock. Yet since Peacock regarded DBS distribution of television as less of a public service than terrestrial distribution, the committee proposed none of the regulation through the IBA that forms part of its Recommendation 10.

Recommendation 15 proposes that 'national telecommunication' systems (i.e. British Telecom and Mercury, but not cable franchises or Hull Telephones) should be permitted to act as common carriers. The intention is to promote the penetration of broadband services by enabling British Telecom (and Mercury) to benefit from the economies of scale and scope that may attend the provision of transmission capacity for telephony and television together. The recommendation seeks to break the impasse in UK cable provision and accelerate its availability. This is a recommendation designed to speed up the provision of an infrastructure for subscription television and the 'electronic publishing' regime advocated by Peacock as a means of augmenting consumer sovereignty, choice and allocative efficiency. We do not share the Peacock judgement on 'electronic publishing' and develop our critique of this strategic dimension of the Peacock report below.

There has been vigorous opposition to the Peacock proposals from the existing terrestrial broadcasters and the government's full response remains, as yet, undefined. However, the Cabinet committee considering the future of broadcasting is reported (*The Financial Times*, 11 September 1986) to be first considering Peacock's proposals to index the BBC licence fee to the RPI, auction ITV franchises, require peritelevision sockets on new televisions and permit Channel Four to sell its own advertising. On 20 November 1986 the Home Secretary Douglas Hurd pronounced on a number of matters that had been the concern of Peacock. He said that all broadcasters in the UK should, within four years, acquire 25 percent of their programmes from independent producers and that, should the Conservative Party be elected (as it was in June 1987), competitive tendering for ITV franchises would be introduced by 1993 (*The Financial Times*, 21 November 1986).

The longer-term importance of the Peacock report rests on its notion of consumer sovereignty and its strategic vision of how the broadcasting market might become more sensitive to consumer demands. Few public service broadcasters now make their case against a market system of allocations in broadcasting in terms of the need to protect audiences and guide the ascent of the cultural pyramid by listeners and viewers. Instead, as in the Annan report, diversity is the principal value to which appeal is made. A problem remains — how can you ensure that the diversity of programming offered is the diversity that consumers desire (rather than that producers wish to offer) when there are only the highly imperfect signalling systems of audience research, press comment and consumer letters and telephone calls to indicate demand? The report refers to the impression given by broadcasters 'that the viewer's or listener's main function is to react to a set of choices determined by the broadcasting institutions' (para. 577). It emphasizes the broadcasters' reliance on peer evaluations (Prix Italia, Emmys, BAFTA awards and so on) as testimonies to the excellence of their work and quotes a statement by the Director General of the BBC which suggests a 'transmission mentality': 'Broadcasting is not a matter of one person sending a signal to another; or one household to another; it is a process of scattering and thus sowing seed far wide [sic]. Some will fall on stony ground and some on fertile ground. Broadcasting further means that the sower waits to see what grows' (Peacock, 1986a: 130).

If the Peacock Committee's goal of consumer sovereignty and its dissatisfaction with the existing broadcasting institutions in the UK are accepted (and they are not universally agreed), it remains to assess the nature of the broadcasting market Peacock urges and its superiority to the existing broadcasting order. The committee stated its awareness that 'it is very easy to highlight the deficiencies of an existing imperfect system but one must avoid making a false comparison between it and some hypothetical idealised alternative' (para. 203).

The existing order has important achievements to its credit. The IBA has exercised its 'trusteeship' to create an economically healthy industry which, together with the BBC, has consistently returned a positive balance of trade with the rest of the world and which significantly contributes to the 'critical mass' of the UK's cultural industries. The broadcasting institutions are strong enough to annoy government and other important UK power centres, they offer a greater diversity of programming than does the United States' TV system and more entertainment than other European public service systems. Advertising is not as intrusive as in the United States (nor as discreet as in West Germany). British television drama has offered moments of astonishing originality and power — *Out, Driving Ambition, Boys From the Blackstuff*. But the industry has successfully evaded levy payments to the Treasury. Major social groups in the UK are dissatisfied with their representation on television and the absence of their voice in broadcasting. Broadcasters are unaccountable to consumers — viewers and listeners who enjoy no mechanisms of influence, control or redress over the broadcasting system or broadcasters that claim to serve them. There is, we judge, a case to answer. Peacock's scepticism of the claims of the existing order to perpetuate itself and proposal to establish as a central principle as far as is possible consumer sovereignty rather than authority (acting as trustee for the public interest) deserves more sympathetic attention and constructive criticism than it has yet received.

The essence of the Peacock case is that a competitive market maximizes welfare and that conditions exist in which, if not a perfect market, an approximation superior to the existing administered regime may be achieved. Both propositions are contestable and we have addressed the question of how far the broadcast market can practise competition (and the cost of competition) extensively earlier in this study. Peacock's case for competition in the broadcasting market is a novel one in the UK and advocacy of it is inspired by a perception that technological change can make possible what previously was unachievable. A central element of Peacock's argument is that a crucial policy constraint — scarcity of that central resource for broadcasting, the radio spectrum — has been overcome (see also Brittan, 1987). Both the Pilkington and Annan reports printed diagrams showing allocation and use of the radio spectrum allocation and Pilkington stated that 'broadcasting is dependent upon the availability of suitable radio frequencies' (para. 13). Yet while spectrum scarcity has been a major rationale for an administered regulatory regime for broadcasting in the UK, Pilkington in particular offered rationales for substantial regulation and public sector presence in broadcasting that depend on arguments other than spectrum scarcity.

Technological innovation promises to deliver broadcasting policy from the constraints imposed by spectrum scarcity. New areas of spectrum are being opened to use (notably the centimetric band by satellites), and in some markets broadband cable distribution of television is pervasive, while in others video-cassette recorders have displaced or reordered consumption of broadcast television. These changes are of interest to students of broadcasting policy for two reasons. First, they remove conditions which have acted as barriers to entry to new information providers and potentially therefore to new ideas. Second, new distribution technologies promise not only to abolish scarcity but also to remove the public-good characteristics of terrestrial broadcasting (though satellite broadcasting may still exhibit public-good characteristics), and therefore offer the possibility of establishing competition in broadcasting services.

The Peacock Committee's main conclusion was identified by Samuel Brittan (1986: 1) as 'British broadcasting should move to a sophisticated market system, based on consumer sovereignty'. Brittan added, 'The most likely route to the full broadcasting market is the development of an optic fibre network.' Such technological change will deliver release from market failure and promises to deliver for broadcasting what the technological change of printing by movable types did for the book. The analogy with printing is one to which the Peacock Committee returns again and again. The committee recognized that neither an advertising-financed television nor the UK public service model of governance by authority delivered consumer sovereignty and argued (para. 606) that 'the most likely route to the full broadcasting market is the development of an optic fibre network by the telecommunications industry'.

This 'electronic publishing', a neologism the committee attributes to Peter Jay, is conditional on a 'national grid of infinite channel capacity based upon fibre optics' (para. 493) which would connect 'every household in the country, whereby the nation's viewers could simultaneously watch as many different programmes as the nation's readers can simultaneously read different books, magazines, newspapers etc.' (para. 481). The committee's espousal of Jay's proposal is extraordinary. Penetration of basic telephony in the UK (service on considerably lower cost than the broadband system advocated by Jay and Peacock) has reached only 79.2 percent of households (British Telecom, 1986: 28). It was widely recognized during the last outbreak of technological frenzy in the UK (which was prompted by the ITAP report *Cable Systems*, 1982) that cable was likely to serve at most only 50 percent of UK households. And there is considerable scepticism that even the bandwidth increase to 64 kbits per second that will attend the introduction of ISDN (integrated services digital network) will ever be required by domestic users. The costs of the Jay model are likely to far exceed its benefits. Though imperfect competition prevails in existing broadcast markets — whether the 'comfortable duopoly' of the UK or the advertising-financed system of the United States — they deliver television to viewers very cheaply. The cost of alternatives to broadcast television that are 'public good' proof (i.e. do not permit free-riding) and have the desired characteristic of responsiveness to fluctuations in demand and supply may be so high as to price the new delivery systems out of the market. This is by no means a purely theoretical concern. The cost of cable subscriptions in the USA is sufficiently high to have prompted substantial numbers of subscribers to disconnect from systems, and cable-theft (unauthorized and unpaid-for reception of cable signals) is in some franchises 50 percent of authorized subscriptions. Rendering the networks more theft-proof (a transaction cost) raises the price of the service, providing a greater incentive for theft and disconnection. So pervasive has cable-theft become that it was the basis for a recent episode of *Hill Street Blues*.

Scrambled transmission of broadcast television signals in the USA — intelligible only with rental (or illegal purchase or construction) of a decoder — has proved an unattractive and excessively costly means of delivering information. Wometco Home Theater (WHT), for example, transmitted a single channel of feature films in scrambled form in the greater Philadelphia area from 1982 to 1984. WHT charged subscribers $24.95 per month and an additional $3.95 per month for late-night 'adult' films. Subscribers declined from 20,000 in 1982 to 4400 in November 1984 when the service was terminated. Such subscription services require, it is estimated, 60,000 subscribers in order to break even, and between 1982 and 1984 sixteen such services ceased operation in the United States (*Philadelphia Inquirer*, 28 November 1984, p. 91).

The publishing market that is canvassed by Jay as a model is imperfectly competitive. There are, it is true, many fewer barriers to entry than exist in the broadcast market, but there is pervasive abuse of market power within the publishing and printing markets. Markets in information and communications have few of the characteristics that distinguish competitive markets. The problem of lack of competition and consumer sovereignty in broadcasting that Peacock identifies and addresses is pervasive, as we have argued, in mass communications.

The model of print publishing is an unfortunate one for the Peacock Committee to have chosen. While the recent lowering of barriers to entry to the UK newspaper market has been attended by the publication of several new titles, the UK newspaper business exhibits few of the characteristics of the free market-place of ideas and consumer sovereignty desired by Peacock. Nor is the printing industry a good model. Oligopolistic tendencies there are causing a restructuring that 'is wiping out the middle range printing group . . . and concentrating a far higher proportion of production in the top ten companies' (*The Financial Times*, 24 November 1986, p. 23).

But the committee's critique of the existing broadcasting order and its regime of 'authorities' is salutary and persuasive. Its recommendations for improvement of the productive efficiency of UK broadcasting are pertinent and should reduce costs. It is important to recognize that the report's section on improvements in productive efficiency is very short — pages 120–3 — and suffers from the pervasive difficulty experienced by broadcasting policy researchers that little information is in the public domain and the broadcasters with the information have an interest in keeping it private.) But the committee's grand strategy of approximating broadcasting in the UK to the condition of print publishing is badly flawed.

There are real possibilities for improving consumer sovereignty and allocative efficiency unexplored by Peacock. They involve the creation of new political institutions for the regulation of broadcasting. It is customarily forgotten that the 'Victorian values' often invoked by reforming free marketeers included the promiscuous invention of new political institutions and a reformed political order. Though the Peacock Committee's report does not consider such developments, its iconoclastic assault on the existing authorities and championship of consumer sovereignty offers a more helpful context for the posing of such questions and the orchestration of the necessary and too-long postponed change in British broadcasting than has existed before. That is a notable achievement and one for which the Peacock Committee has been given too little credit.

The authors of this study differ in their evaluation of the Peacock analysis and proposals. They share a judgement that the broadcasting market is imperfect and that acceptance of its imperfections is to be preferred to the alternative of creating a very expensive infrastructure of 'electronic publishing', the market for which is likely to be far from perfect. But differ in their evaluation of the achievement of the established British broadcasters. Our view is that terrestrial broadcasting, though imperfect, is less worse than the costly system of 'electronic publishing' advocated by Peacock. We differ though in our views on whether the existing system is to be characterized as a 'comfortable duopoly' captured by 'outsiders'. Accordingly, we differ in our evaluation of a number of Peacock's specific proposals, for example, on financially disciplining the BBC or the role of independent producers. But exploration of those issues would require a book on the politics of television in the UK — a project rather different from this study, though one which could well take as its starting point Professor

Peacock's statement that 'economic policy is too important a matter to be left to economists' (Peacock, 1979: 22).

References

Adam Smith Institute (1984) *The Omega File*. London: Adam Smith Institute.

Alvarado, M. and Stewart, J. (1985) *Made for Television: Euston Films Limited*. London: British Film Institute.

Ang, I. (1985) 'The Battle between Television and its Audiences: the Politics of Watching Television', in P. Drummond and R. Paterson (eds.) *Television in Transition*. London: British Film Institute.

Annan, Lord (chairman) (1977) *Report of the Committee on the Future of Broadcasting*. Cmnd 6753. London: HMSO.

Bank of England (1985) *Quarterly Bulletin*, September. London.

Barnett S. (1986) 'Pricing the Radio Spectrum'. Broadcasting Research Unit Working Paper. London: Broadcasting Research Unit.

Baumol, H. and Baumol, W.J. (1976) 'The Mass Media and the Cost Disease', in W.S. Hendon, H. Horowitz and C.R. Waits (eds.) *Economics of Cultural Industries*. Akron, Ohio: Association for Cultural Economics.

Baumol, W.J., Blackman, S.A.B. and Wolff, E.N. (1984) *Unbalanced Growth Revisited: Asymptotic Stagnancy and New Evidence*. New York: C.V. Starr Centre for Applied Economics, New York University, Faculty of Arts and Science.

Baumol, W.J. and Bowen, W.G. (1966) *Performing Arts: the Economic Dilemma*. New York: Twentieth Century Fund.

BBC (British Broadcasting Corporation) *BBC Annual Report and Handbook*. London: BBC.

BBC *BBC Television: Facts and Figures* (annually). London: BBC.

Blanchard, S. (1983) *Film and Video Distribution and Exhibition in London*. London: Greater London Council.

British Telecom (1986) *Supplementary Report*. London.

Brittan, S. (1986) 'Bird's Eye View of Peacock', *The Financial Times*, 5 July.

Brittan, S. (1987) 'The Myth of Spectrum Shortage', *The Financial Times*, 16 April.

Broadcast (weekly). London.

Broadcasting (weekly). New York.

Broadcasting Act, 1981. London: HMSO.

BRU (Broadcasting Research Unit) (1983) *A Report from the Working Party on the New Technologies*. London: Broadcasting Research Unit.

Burns, M. and Walsh, C. (1981) 'Market Provision of Price-Excludable Public Goods: a General Analysis', *Journal of Political Economy*, 1: 166–91.

Business Monitor (quarterly). London.

Business Week (weekly). New York.

Cable and Broadcasting Act 1984. London: HMSO.

Cable and Satellite Europe [previously *Cable and Satellite News*] (monthly). London.

Cave, M. (1984) 'Broadcasting Regulation and the New Technologies'. Australian National University Centre for Economic Policy.

Cave, M. (1985) 'Financing British Broadcasting', *Lloyds Bank Review*, July.
Cave, M. and Swann, P. (1985) *The Effects on Advertising Revenues of Allowing Advertising on BBC Television*. London: HMSO.
Channel Four Television *Report and Accounts* (annually). London.
Chapman, G. (1987) 'Towards a Geography of the Tube: TV Flows in Western Europe', *Intermedia*, 15(1): 10–21.
Collins, R. (1986) 'Wall to Wall "Dallas"? The US–UK Trade in Television', *Screen*, 27(3–4): 66–77.
Commission of the European Communities (1984) *Television Without Frontiers*. Green Paper on the establishment of the Common Market for broadcasting, especially by satellite and cable. COM (84) 300 final. Luxembourg: Office for Official Publications of the European Communities.
Comptroller and Auditor General (1985) *Independent Broadcasting Authority: Additional Payments by Programme Contractors*. London: HMSO.
Connell, S. (1985) 'Information Dissemination by Satellite', *Le Bulletin de l'IDATE*. Montpellier: IDATE.
Cyert, R.M. and March, J.G. (1963) *A Behavioural Theory of the Firm*. Englewood Cliffs, NJ: Prentice-Hall.
Domberger, S. and Middleton, J. (1985) 'Franchising in Practice: the Case of Independent Television in the UK', *Fiscal Studies*, 6: 17–33.
Ehrenberg, A. and Barwise, P. (1982) *How Much Does UK Television Cost?* London: London Business School.
FCC (Federal Communications Commission) (1980) *New Television Networks: Entry, Jurisdiction, Ownership and Regulation*. Washington, DC: FCC.
Gellhorn, E. and Pierce, R. (1982) *Regulated Industries*. St Paul, MN: Nutshell Books.
Goodhart, D. and Wintour, P. (1986) *Eddie Shah and the Newspaper Revolution*. London: Coronet Books.
Greater London Council (1982) *Cabling in London*. London: GLC.
Greater London Council (1983) 'Report on GLC/Sheffield City Council Hearings', July. London: GLC.
Greater London Council (1984) *London Industrial Strategy: Cable*. London: GLC.
Greater London Council (1985) *The State of the Art or the Art of the State?* London: GLC.
Greater London Enterprise Board (1985) 'Altered Images: towards a Strategy for London's Cultural Industries'. Sector Strategy Series: Reshaping London's Industries, 3. London: GLEB.
Grieve Horner and Associates (n.d.) 'A Study of the United States Market for Television Programs'. Toronto. (A consultants' report probably produced in 1981.)
Haley, Sir William (1948) 'The Lewis Fry Memorial Lecture', in A. Smith (ed) *British Broadcasting*. Newton Abbot: David and Charles.
Home Office (1981) *Direct Broadcasting by Satellite*. London: HMSO.
Home Office (1986) *A Review of the ITV and ILR Levy Structures 1984–85*. Report of a Working Group of Officials of the Home Office, Treasury and IBA.
Home Office (1987) *Radio: Choices and Opportunities*. London: HMSO.
Hoskins, C. and McFadyen, S. (1986) 'Stimulation of National Television Program Production: A Canadian Success Story?' Paper presented to the International Television Studies Conference, London.

Houghton, R.W. (ed.) (1970) *Public Finance*. Harmondsworth: Penguin.

House of Lords (1985) *Television Without Frontiers*. Report of the Select Committee on the European Communities. HL43. London: HMSO.

IBA (Independent Broadcasting Authority) *Annual Report and Accounts*. London: IBA.

IBA *Television and Radio: Yearbook of Independent Broadcasting*. London: IBA.

IBA (1985) *Evidence to the Committee on Financing the BBC*. London: IBA.

ITAP (Information Technology Advisory Panel) (1982) *Cable Systems*. London: HMSO.

ITCA (Independent Television Contractors Association) (1985) *ITV Evidence to the Peacock Committee*. London: Independent Television Contractors Association.

Katz, E. and Liebes, T. (1985) 'Mutual Aid in the Decoding of *Dallas*: Preliminary Notes from a Cross-Cultural Study', in P. Drummond and R. Paterson (eds.) *Television in Transition*. London: British Film Institute.

Marris, R. and Müller, D.C. (1980) 'The Corporation, Competition and the Invisible Hand', *Journal of Economic Literature*, 18(1): 32–63.

Merriman, J.H.H. (chairman) (1984) *Report of the Independent Review of the Radio Spectrum*. 30–960 MHZ. Cmnd 9000. London: HMSO.

Miège, B., Pajon, P. and Salaun, J.M. (1986) *L'Industralisation de l'Individual*. Paris: Autur.

Mills, P. (1985) 'An International Audience?', *Media, Culture and Society*, 7(4): 487–502.

Nath, S.K. (1973) *A Perspective of Welfare Economics*. London: Macmillan.

National Audit Office (1985) *Independent Broadcasting Authority Additional Payments by Programme Contractors*. Report by the Comptroller and Auditor General. London: HMSO.

NEDO (National Economic Development Office) (1984) *The Crisis facing UK Information Technology*. London: NEDO.

NERA (National Economic Research Associates) (1985) *The Effects on Other Media of the Introduction of Advertising on the BBC*. London: HMSO.

Nielson, E. (chairman) (1986) *Economic Growth, Culture and Communications*. A Study Team Report to the Task Force on Program Policy. Ottawa: Ministry of Supply and Services.

Nordenstreng, K. and Varis, T. (1974) *Television Traffic: a One-way Street?* Paris: UNESCO.

OECD (Organization for Economic Co-operation and Development) (1986) *OECD Observer* 141 (July).

Owen, B.M., Beebe, J.H. and Manning, W.G. (1974) *Television Economics*. Lexington, MA: Lexington Books.

Peacock, A. (1979) *The Economic Analysis of Government*. Oxford: Martin Robertson.

Peacock, A. (chairman) (1986a) *Report of the Committee on Financing the BBC*. Cmnd 9824. London: HMSO.

Peacock, A. (1986b) 'Television Tomorrow'. Paper presented to the International Institute of Communication Conference Edinburgh. (Revised version published as 'Technology, the Political Economy of Broadcasting', *Intermedia* 14(6), 1986: 35–7.)

Peat, Marwick, Mitchell and Co. (1985) 'BBC: Value for Money'. Unpublished report, January.

Phillips, W. (1986) 'The State of the Teleconomics', *Broadcast* 19 Nov.

Pilkington, H. (chairman) (1962) *Report of the Committee on Broadcasting (1960)*. Cmnd 1753. London: HMSO.

Radio Regulatory Division (1986) *Department of Trade and Industry Annual Report 1985/86*. London: Department of Trade and Industry.

Ravault, R.J. (1980) 'De l'exploitation des "despotes culturels" par les téléspectateurs', in A. Méar (ed.) *Recherches Québécoises sur la télévision*. Montréal: Editions Albert St Martin.

Rowley, C. and Peacock, A. (1975) *Welfare Economics: a Liberal Restatement*. Oxford: Martin Robertson.

Sepstrup, P. (1985) 'Information Content in TV Advertising', *Journal of Consumer Policy*, 8: Neuweid: Leuchterhand Verlag.

Smith, A. (ed.) (1974) *British Broadcasting*. Newton Abbot: David and Charles.

Steiner, P. O. (1961) 'Monopoly and Competition in Television: some Policy Issues', *The Manchester School*: 107–31.

Television (monthly). Journal of the Royal Television Society. London.

Televizio (weekly). Hilversum: AVRO.

TV World (ten times a year). London.

Veljanovski, C. and Bishop, W.D. (1983) *Choice by Cable – the Economics of a New Era in TV*. London: Institute of Economic Affairs.

Variety (weekly). New York.

Varis, T. (1974) 'The Global Traffic in Television', *Journal of Communication*, 24(1): 102–9.

Varis, T. (1984) 'The International Flow of Television Programs', *Journal of Communication*, 34(1): 143–52.

Vogel, H.L. (1986) *Entertainment Industry Economics*. Cambridge: Cambridge University Press.

Wade, G. (1985) *Film, Video and Television*. London: Comedia.

Winch, D.W. (1971) *Analytical Welfare Economics*. Harmondsworth: Penguin.

Index

ABC network 72, 78
accountability, of broadcasters 124
adult education programmes 40, 42–3
advantage, comparative 51–5, 57–8, 76, 78
advertising: amount of 16, 118; and BBC 5,
  103–4, 111, 118; and EEC 85–6, 92–6; and
  production costs 16, 20; impact of vii, 92,
  101–2, 105–10, 123–4; net advertising
  revenue (NAR) 38–9, 40, 79–81; origin 83
alcohol, advertising 86
Alvarado, Manuel, and Stewart, John 38, 41
Anglia TV: exports 66–7; programming 39
Annan Committee 2, 113–14, 123, 124
ATV 74, 75
auction, for spectrum access 99–100, 121
Australia: exports to 63–4; state support for
  television 52
authority, concept of 114–17, 124–5, 127

Bank of England 61, 62
Barnett, S. 99, 100
Baumol, H., and Baumol, W.J. 16, 18
BBC: consumer costs 15; co-productions 68–
  9, 70; distribution 12–13; funding 5, 111,
  117–18, see also advertising, licence fee;
  labour costs 33, 35–7, 120; new
  programmes 25, 32–4, 35, 36–7;
  organization and control 14; Peacock
  Committee on 111; privatization of radio
  channels 118–19, 121; production costs 16,
  17, 22–3, 24–5, 28, 30, 31–8, 40, 42–3;
  programme exports 63–4, 65, 73, 82;
  programme imports 82–4; regional
  programming 28, 32; structure 10, 26
BBC Enterprises 63–4, 68, 73–4, 82
Belgium, consumer choice 109
Berlusconi, Silvio 89
boards, governing, of television authorities
  116–17
Border TV, programming 39
breakfast television 35
British Aerospace 90–1
British Business 62, 65, 83
British Telecom, Peacock proposals
  122
Brittan, Samuel 112, 113, 125
broadcasting: macroeconomic structure 5,
  10–19; microeconomics of 5–10
Broadcasting Act, 1981 43, 79
Broadcasting Research Unit vi
BSB consortium 91

cable TV 4–5, 12, 87–9, 91, 96, 104, 109, 122,
  124–5; and consumer choice 106; costs 126
Campaign for Press and Broadcasting
  Freedom vi
Canada: and co-productions 69; state support
  for television 52–3
car radios, licence fee on 119
Cave, M. 101
CBS 71, 72
Central TV: advertising revenues 81; co-
  productions 67, 71; exports 65, 75;
  programming 38–9
Channel Four 2, 10; advertising revenues 44,
  118, 121, 122; control 47; co-productions
  69–70; financing 22, 43–4, 48, 121; news 39,
  44–5; production costs 25, 29–30, 43–9;
  programme imports 83–4; programme
  origination 26–7; sales 38
Channel TV: programming 39; sales 38
channels: foreign, reception 86–8; number of
  18, 100, 105, 106–7, 109
children: programmes for, BBC 36, 42–3,
  Channel Four 47; ITV 40–1, 42–3;
  protection of 85–6
Children's Channel 88
choice, consumer 4, 11, 18, 102, 104–5, 106–7,
  109–10, 112, 115–16
Cockfield, Lord 85–6
commercials: origin 83; transmissions 26
communications sovereignty 55–6, 60, 95
competition: in broadcasting market viii, 3, 7,
  13, 100, 104, 106, 110, 111–12, 116, 117,
  121–2; in broadcasting market, imperfect
  viii, 20, 55; international 18, 22, 24; non-
  price 14–15, 16–17, 24
Conservative Party, moral regulation of
  broadcasting 120
consumer preference, *see* choice,
  consumer
consumer sovereignty 4, 111, 114, 117, 122,
  123–7
co-production: international 25, 53, 67–71,
  75–6, 81; UK 47, 62
copyright laws, and EEC 85, 96
Cosgrove Hall 41
costs: consumption 15, 18; inflation 16–18,
  20–2, 76–7, 79; labour 18, 35–7, 41–2;
  marginal 8–9, 35, 48, 53–4, 57, 73, 76, 101;
  opportunity 98
costs of television production 11, 15–16, 18–
  19, 20–49, 73–4, 76–7, 79; and quality 23–6;

comparisons 5, 22–3, 30; control of 4, 20, 22, 35; *see also* quality, and costs
culture, national 55–6, 96–7
current affairs: BBC 26, 35, 36, 42–3; Channel Four 45–6; costs 35, 36; ITV 26, 40–1, 42–3

'*Dallas*, wall-to-wall' 50, 57, 97; *see also* internationalization of television
Dankert, Pieter 95–6
daytime television 35
DBS, *see* satellite TV
DBS consortium 91
DBS UK consortium 91
Debauve case 93, 94
demand, final 4, 15, 57, 58–9
Direct Broadcasting by Satellite 90
distribution: control 12–13; and new technologies 4–5, 18, 85, 87–8, 114, 124–5
documentaries: BBC 36, 42–3, 68; Channel Four 46–7; ITV 40–1, 42–3
Domberger, Simon, and Middleton, Julian 39
drama: BBC 36, 42–3, 50, 68, 69, 124; Channel Four 45–7; ITV 42–3, 75, 124
Drei Sat 88
Dukes, Justin 70
'dumping' in information markets 58, 76

economics, neglect of in broadcasting policy 2
ECSI 88
editors, role of 12, 47
education programmes: BBC 36; Channel Four 46
EEC, and UK television 23, 59, 85–7, 92–7, *see also Television Without Frontiers*
Ehrenberg, A., and Barwise, P. 15
elitism, in broadcasting output 2, 102, 107
Europe, and co-productions 69–70
European Broadcasting Union (EBU) 70
European Satellite Television Broadcasting Corporation 89
Euston Films 41, 71
exclusion 8, 88, 101, 106
exports, television programmes 29, 51–4, 60–7, 79–82

features: BBC 36; Channel Four 47; ITV 40–1, 42–3
fictions, long-running 57
Film on Four International (FFI) 29
films, feature: consumption 103; cost 26, 84; on Channel Four 26–7, 29, 45–6
financing of broadcasting, alternatives, *see* advertising; licence fee; Pay TV
foreign nationals, and ownership of franchises 120
format sales 65, 72–3, 79, 82
Fox network 76–7
franchise, competitive tendering for 119–20, 122, *see also* IBA
'Francophonie, La' 55, 96

Gershman, Lawrence 75–6

goods, cultural 7–9, 10, 54, 58–9, 101, 125–6, *see also* internationalization of television
Grampian TV, programming 39
Granada TV: advertising revenue 81; exports 65–6, 67; programming 38–9
Grand Central Productions 72–3, 79, 82
Greater London Council, research on broadcasting vi
Greater London Enterprise Board vi

Halliwell, Leslie 44
HBO (Home Box Office) 12, 14, 72
Henry, Harry 16
Holland, consumer choice 109
Horner, Grieve 77
Hoskins, C., and McFadyen, S. 52–3
House of Lords Select Committee, 1985 86–7, 92, 93–7
HTV company: exports 66; pre-sales 71; programming 39
Hurd, Douglas 122

IBA: and franchises 22, 26, 29, 42–3, 74, 99–100, 120; levy 16, 22, 29, 78–82, 99; programme imports 82–4; structure 10, 26, 123
immateriality of broadcasting product 7, 10
imperialism, cultural 55–6, 57–8
Independent Television Companies Association (ITCA) 39, 40, 45, 62; co-productions 70–1; television programme exports 65–7, 81–2
Independent Television News (ITN) 39, 44; and satellite TV 91
infant industry argument 52–3
innovation, need for 9–10
Intelsat 5 88
interest groups, pressure from 113
internationalization of television 29, 50–97; cultural advantage 55–6, 57, 81–2, 85, 97; economic advantage 51–4, 57–60
intervention, state 3–4, 6–8, 52–3, 98, 100
ISDN (integrated services digital network) 125
Italy, production costs 24
ITV: advertising revenue 38; consumer costs 15; income 21; labour costs 41–2; production costs 22–3, 24–5, 28–30, 38–43; programme tariff system 39–41; structure 10, 26

Janovskis, Inta 69
Japan: DBS 89; programme exports 54
Jay, Peter 6, 12, 109, 125

Katz, E., and Liebes, T. 58
Kaufman, Gerald 111

labour: intensity of 16–17; international division of 50–1, 54, 57
Labour Party, and ownership of franchises 120

Lang, Jack 50
language, national, and internationalization of television 55, 57
Levinson, Charles 92
levy, IBA 16, 22, 29, 78–82, 99
licence, colour/monochrome 21, 33–4
licence fee 101–3; and public utilities commission 21; as coercive 3; exemptions 119; indexation 20, 21, 119, 122; pressure on 20–1; United States networks 77–8
light entertainment: BBC 36, 42–3; ITV 40–1, 42–3
LWT company: advertising revenue 81; co-productions 67; exports 65–6; programming 38–9; sales 38

market, barriers to entry 5, 16, 58, 99, 109, 126
Maxwell, Robert 89–90
Mercury, Peacock proposals 122
Merriman review 99
Mersey Television 47
Mexico, programme exports 54, 64
Midlands TV 79
Miège, B., et al. 11
'mini-series' 50, 75, 78, 84
minorities, programme choice 13, 104–5
monopoly, and market imperfection 3, 16
morality, and regulation of broadcasting 111, 120
Murdoch, Rupert 77, 108
Music Box 88, 92

National Economic Research Associates (NERA) 79
NBC network 71, 72
NBS consortium 91
network companies, UK 39–40
networks, United States 13, 14, 69, 76–8
newspapers, compared with television 100, 107–9, 126
Nielson report, Canada 53
novelty of broadcasting product 7, 9–10, 13

Open University broadcasts 28, 43
optic fibres, use of 125
organization and control 13–14
outside broadcasts, ITV 40–1

Pareto, V.F.D. 2–3, 8, 101
Parkin, Byron 68–9
Pay TV 13, 15, 77, 88, 101–2, 105–10, 122
PBS stations, United States 45, 67, 72, 75, 77
Peacock, Alan vi, 2, 3, 98, 111–12, 128
Peacock Committee 1, 6; advertising finance vii, viii, 20; assessment of 117–28; on cable 111; on competition 121–2; impact of 111, 123–4; on Pay TV 106–7; and public service requirement 99–100, 112–13, 117; radicalism viii, 112–13, 114–15, 117; remit vi, 1–2, 5, 111
Peat, Marwick, Mitchell 17, 24, 34, 35

Pilkington report, 1962 111, 114–17, 124
piracy 13
'pre-sales' 62, 67–70, 71, 75
price mechanism 7–8, 14–15, 98–100, 106
production: independent 12, 30, 44–9, 86, 112; Peacock proposals 20, 22, 121, 122; provincial 55
productivity, broadcasting 16–18, 48–9
programmes: acquired 25–7, 30, 35, 37, 41, 44–5, 49, 82–4, 109, *see also* internationalization; networked 39, 40
property rights, 98, 100
public goods, *see* goods, cultural
public service broadcasting: and choice 107; and national culture 97; and price mechanism 99–100, 111; support for 113–16, 124
Public Service Broadcasting Council 112–13
publishing, electronic 122, 125, 127

quality: and costs 23–6, 29; UK television 1, 14
quota: European production 23, 86; imported programmes 82–3

radio: BBC 28, 31; independent local 121; privatization 118–19, 121
Radio: Choices and Opportunities, Green Paper vii
Radio Regulatory Division 98–9
RAI, Italy 70, 88, 107
Ravault, R.J. 59
reception, satellite TV 91
religion: BBC 36, 42–3; Channel Four 46; ITV 40–1, 42–3
repeats, use of 13, 17, 18, 27, 35, 109
reply, right of 85, 86, 96
research and development 9–10
resources, allocation: efficiency 2, 4, 23–4, 38, 48, 118, 127; price system 7–8, 10; *see also* spectrum; values
Ricardo, David 51
Rowley, Chris 74
Rowley, C. and Peacock, A. 1, 3

S4C: advertising revenues 118; production costs 25
Saatchi case 93, 94
sales: profitability 73–8, *see also* format sales; 'pre-sales'; trade
SAT UK consortium 91
satellite TV: 'direct broadcasting' 88–92, 95–6, 104, 109, 122; and distribution 4–5, 87–8, 108, 124–5; financing 91; impact of vii, 18, 50, 92
scale, economies of 8–9, 11, 14, 16, 18, 23, 25, 36–7, 108, *see also* internationalization of television
scheduling, of programmes 23, 25–6, 42, 111–12
Schmerz, Herb 67

schools broadcasts: BBC 26, 42–3; ITV 26, 40–1, 42–3
scope, economies of 11–12, 16, 23, 53
Scottish TV, programming 39
scrambling, of TV signals 8, 88, 101, 126
second-best, concept of 101
Sepstrup, P. 92
Showtime 72
Sky Channel 88, 91, 92, 93–4
SMATV systems 87
spectrum, scarcity 5, 98–100, 104, 106, 110, 121, 124
sports programmes 13–14, 35, 36–7, 39; BBC 36–7, 42–3; Channel Four 45–7; ITV 39, 40–1, 42–3
Starstream consortium 91
strategies: flow-culture 11, 12–13; multi-channel 12; network programming 12, 13, 14
stripping, programme 72, 75
Subscription TV, *see* Pay TV
subsidiaries, ITV 41, 67
subsidy: cross-subsidy 11, 39–40; programme 39, 52–3
Super Channel 88, 91, 92
Survival Anglia Ltd, exports 66
syndication 18, 69, 72, 75, 77

Taurus Films 89
taxation 102, *see also* licence fee
TDF1, France 89
telecommunications, Peacock proposals 122, 125
Television Without Frontiers viii, 70, 85–7, 92–7
Thames Television: advertising revenue 79–81; co-productions 67, 82; exports 38, 65, 67, 72–3, 75; imports 84; programming 38–9; and satellite TV 91
time, as factor in distribution 13
tobacco, advertising 86

trade, UK, in television programmes 60–7, 72–82, 84
trade theory, *see* advantage, comparative
transmissions, increase in 34–5, 37
TROS, Holland 107
TSW TV company: programming 39; sales 38
TV5 88, 89
TV-am: programming 39, 83; sales 38
TV Sat 1, West Germany 89
TVS company, programming 39
Tyne Tees TV, programming 39

Ulster TV, programming 39
Unisat 90
United States: consumer choice 105; exports to 74–8; Pay TV 106–7; production costs 16, 17, 24–5, 81; programme exports from 51–4, 58–61

values: and allocation of resources 2–5; and importing of programmes 55–6
variety in programming mix 104–5, 106–7, 115, 121, 123
Varis, T. 58
video-cassette recorders (VCRs), and distribution 4–5, 13, 124
Vogel, H.L. 105–6

welfare economics 2–3, 8, 13, 50, 98, 106, 116, 124
wildlife programmes, BBC 68
Wometco Home Theater (WHT) 126

x-efficiency 14, 20, 23
x-inefficiency 14–15

Yorkshire TV: advertising revenue 81; co-productions 71; exports 66; programming 38–9
Zenith 71, 75, 79, 82
Zweites Deutsches Fernsehen 69, 70